PERSPECTIVES ON THE HISTORY
OF ECONOMIC THOUGHT
VOLUME V

THEMES IN PRE-CLASSICAL, CLASSICAL AND
MARXIAN ECONOMICS

Perspectives on the History of Economic Thought Volume V

Themes in Pre-Classical, Classical and Marxian Economics

Selected Papers from the
History of Economics Conference
1989

Edited by
William J. Barber

Published for the History of Economics Society
by Edward Elgar

Published by
Edward Elgar Publishing Limited
The Lypiatts
15 Lansdown Road
Cheltenham
Glos GL50 2JA
UK

Edward Elgar Publishing, Inc.
William Pratt House
9 Dewey Court
Northampton
Massachusetts 01060
USA

Reprinted 2017

British Library Cataloguing in Publication Data
History of Economics Society (Conference; 1989; Richmond, Va.)
   Themes in pre-classical, classical and Marxian economics :
   selected papers from the History of Economics Conference
   1989. – (Perspectives on the history of economic thought, v. 5).
   1. Economics. Theories, history
   I. Title II. Barber, William J. (William Joseph) *1925*– III. Series
   330.1

Library of Congress Cataloguing-in-Publication Data
History of Economics Society. Conference (1989: University of Richmond)
     Themes in pre-classical, classical, and Marxian economics :
   selected papers from the History of Economics Society Conference,
   1989 / edited by William J. Barber.
     p. cm. – (Perspectives on the history of economic thought; v.5)
     Conference held June 10–13, 1989 in Richmond, Virginia.
     Includes bibliographical references and index.
     1. Classical school of economics–Congresses.   2. Marxian
  economics–Congresses.   I. Barber, William J.   II. Title.   III. Series
  HB94.H57   1989
330.15–dc20   90–14035
                                        CIP

ISBN 978 1 85278 363 1

Printed and bound in Great Britain by the CPI Group (UK) Ltd

Contents

PART IV TOPICS IN THE ECONOMICS OF MARXISM

Introduction

William J. Barber

This volume and its companion – *Perspectives on the History of Economic Thought, Volume VI: Themes in Keynesian Criticism and Supplementary Modern Topics* – continue a publishing programme initiated in 1987. At that time, the officers of the History of Economics Society entered an agreement with Edward Elgar Publishing Ltd to permit the publication of a select group of papers presented at the Society's annual conferences. The essays presented here have been drawn from a pool of more than 120 papers discussed at the sixteenth annual meeting of the History of Economics Society which was held at the University of Richmond, Richmond, Virginia from 10–13 June, 1989. Scholars from 21 countries were in attendance.

Should anyone entertain lingering doubts about the vitality, diversity and ingenuity of current scholarship in the history of economics, a careful reading of the contents of these volumes should dispel them. By any measure – chronological, geographical, methodological – the substantive topics treated span a wide range. This catholicity is deliberate: the intellectual energies in evidence at the 1989 meetings could not otherwise be adequately reflected. Even so, there are features in common. Each of the papers – though often in quite different ways – illustrates how the study of earlier thought can throw light on current controversies or how current analytic approaches can illuminate our understanding of longstanding problems.

At the inevitable risk of an element of arbitrariness, these papers have been divided into four groups. Part I – Pre-Classical Economic Issues – directs our attention to bodies of thought that are all too frequently neglected. Louis Baeck's essay brings to life the economic literature of the age of Classical Islam and, in so doing, opens a window on a world that is closed to all save a few Western scholars. Islamic economic thinkers, as he notes, took the moral injunctions of the Koran – which set out guidelines on taxation and distribution of inherited property and also proscribed lending at interest – as their point of departure. But the era of Islamic imperial expansion and the growth of trade and urbanization that went with it generated new challenges to thinkers concerned about appropriate economic organization. This, in turn, stimulated some noteworthy theorizing about the role of public finance, money, and state intervention in price-setting. Finally, the decline of the Islamic Empire after the mid-thirteenth century inspired original analyses of economic factors underlying long-period historical change.

André Lapidus's re-reading of the thought of medieval schoolmen on the subject of usury provides an interesting counterpoint to one of the themes addressed by Baeck. Whereas Islamic commentators in the period Baeck surveyed adhered strictly to a prohibition of lending at interest, the medieval Christian schoolmen developed a more elastic approach to the analysis of 'usurious' transactions. And this very elasticity has puzzled many scholars who have been inclined to view the position of the church as lacking in consistency. The reasons for such perplexity are understandable. On the one hand, the schoolmen proscribed the stipulation of interest payments in the loan contract; on the other, they found ways to justify repayments to a lender in excess of the capital advanced. Lapidus offers an interpretation which reconciles apparent contradictions by examining the manner in which scholastic thinkers struggled to discriminate between 'licit' and 'illicit' transactions in recognizing usury as a 'sin of intention', rather than a matter of material fact. His investigations of their judgements on the legitimacy of a variety of contracts that were substitutes for formal loans assign to their authors a higher level of analytic sophistication than they have usually been accorded. In particular, they reveal a comprehension of concepts commonly associated with the economics of much later days, for example, concepts of 'opportunity costs', of the difference between present and future values, of risk-bearing and its incidence, and of asymmetry of information.

Todd Lowry's contribution prompts reflection on the nature of the fundamental shift in the Western mentality concerning economic 'rationality' and ethical 'individualism' marked by the publication of Adam Smith's *Wealth of Nations*. As he notes, the earlier traditions of thought – rooted in the texts of the ancient world which resurfaced in the Renaissance – were linked with an élitist conception of the social order. The 'individual' was the leader who had a moral obligation to administer the affairs of the community in the common interest. What passed for writing on 'political economy' was largely a body of literature designed to instruct the leader on the rational conduct of public affairs. As Lowry reminds us, the notion that economic rationality could be 'democratized' in the marketplace and that economic affairs could be administered by an 'invisible hand' entered the stage only at a recent moment in historical time. He suggests, moreover, that some manifestations of the early 'élitist' tradition – with its emphasis on the efficiency and administrative skill of an individual – may still survive in the prestige enjoyed by successful entrepreneurs.

Part II opens with Antoin Murphy's reassessment of the thought of John Law, a figure whose place in the stream of monetary macroeconomic thinking has long been in dispute. The facts about Law's career, to be sure, have been adequately established – in particular, his daring approach to the note issue which was translated into official policy in France in the early eighteenth century. Murphy adds to our knowledge by demonstrating the way Law drew upon his observations of the practices of the Bank of England and the English East India Company in developing a 'grand design' for collaterizing the French note issue against such 'assets' as the overseas trading monopolies. In addition, this essay demonstrates that an appreciation of the problems of public debt management in France is central to an understanding of the rationale underlying Law's operations. When identifying the fatal flaw in the 'grand design', Murphy suggests that the economic policy-makers of Revolutionary France in the 1790s – when analogous monetary and debt management problems had to be addressed – could usefully have learned from Law's mistakes.

An issue that has been much debated for the better part of a century is studied with new techniques in the contribution of Mary Ann Dimand and Robert W. Dimand. 'Das Adam Smith Problem' – so named by German scholars who addressed this topic in the 1890s – turns on whether or not the behavioural presuppositions underpinning Smith's *Theory of Moral Sentiments* (published in 1759) can be reconciled with those of *The Wealth of Nations* (published in 1776). In short, is there an inconsistency between the emphasis Smith assigned to 'altruism' in the earlier document and to the doctrine of 'self interest' developed in the later one? Over the years, various answers have been given to this question. Combining the techniques of textual analysis with those of mathematical modelling, the Dimands show that a consistency can be demonstrated, arguing that the presence of moral sentiments in market behaviour is compatible with general competitive equilibrium as it is formally understood in modern micro theory.

John Vint also brings some modern analytic tools to bear – in this case, methodological ones – in the reinterpretation of a classical problem. The issue centres on the controversy about the 'wages fund'. This doctrine asserted that the savings of capitalists supplied the resources to support the hiring of workers. As at any particular moment this 'fund' had a predetermined size, it followed that the wage rate would be established by dividing the 'fund' by the number of workers. Two implications appeared to follow. First, growth in the labour force through population increase would reduce the wage rate; and second, efforts on the part of workers to raise wages would result in unemployment. But there was an ambiguity about whether the 'fund' should be conceptualized in real terms or in money terms. Using the Lakatosian approach to scientific research programmes, Vint examines the strategies deployed to defend the hard core of the doctrine from challenge and offers an account of John Stuart Mill's intellectual journey which led to recantation of his earlier support for this doctrine.

Part III develops two novel approaches to British controversies over money and banking in the nineteenth century. Thomas Humphrey links the structure of those earlier arguments with matters of lively analytic contention in the late twentieth century. In his reading, Milton Friedman's monetarism can be seen as the modern heir to the doctrines espoused by the Bullionist and the Currency schools in the earlier period. Similarly, the contours of Nicholas Kaldor's neo-Keynesian anti-monetarism were anticipated by the advocates of the anti-bullionist and Banking school positions of more than a century ago.

Timothy Alborn's essay is an exercise in cross-disciplinary and cross-professional comparisons. In the first instance, he draws an analogy between dominant attitudes in early nineteenth century Britain towards the 'wealth of nations', allegedly promoted by faith in the natural order and the invisible hand; and towards the 'health of nations', presumably best assured when individual medical practitioners administered therapy on the basis of practical experience. Both commercial bankers and doctors took this to mean that they should be free to conduct their affairs without governmental interference. Alborn traces the way in which the professional autonomy of both groups was subsequently challenged by the rise of a 'science' claiming superior insight into the workings of the human body and body economic. Ricardian economics and the support it lent to Peel's bank legislation threatened the bankers; studies in anatomical theory, and later in bacteriology, redefined professionalism in the medical world at the expense of the practitioners who had heavily based their claims to competence on accumulated experience in the bedside manner. Alborn identifies a number of striking parallels between the strategies adopted by both groups.

Part IV introduces two topics pertaining to Marxian economics and presents perspectives that are not readily available in published form elsewhere. Zoltan Kenessey provides an arresting insight into the question of why *Das Kapital* was unfinished at the time of Marx's death. His researches in the archival materials housed in Amsterdam have revealed that Marx had a keen interest in investigating the mathematical laws of the business cycle and that he accumulated a considerable amount of statistical material with that end in view. This dimension of Marx's interest received scant attention in the published versions of Volumes II and III, edited by Engels from the materials Marx left behind. Kenessey argues that the project Marx set for himself was beyond his reach, given the inadequacy of data and of computational facilities available to him. Nevertheless the aspiration to bring this line of inquiry to a successful resolution may well account, at least in part, for Marx's failure to complete his overall programme. This conclusion, as the author acknowledges, is necessarily conjectural. Even so, the evidence brought to light about Marx's interest in mathematical–statistical methods of analysis is itself refreshingly instructive.

Johan Lönnroth examines the fate of Marxian doctrine in Sweden, the country known by the mid-twentieth century as the representative specimen of 'the middle way' in economic organization and policy. In the last half of the nineteenth century, a number of figures in the nascent workers' movement attempted to adapt Marxian arguments drawn from the labour theory of value to mobilize their constituency in protest against capitalist 'exploitation'. Why then did a Marxian version of socialism not enjoy greater success? Lönnroth traces part of the answer to the interventions of Swedish economists who were ultimately to become major international figures: among them, Knut Wicksell and Gustav Cassell in the late nineteenth and early twentieth centuries and subsequently, Gunnar Myrdal and Assar Lindbeck. At crucial points in their careers, each was regarded as sympathetic to some form of socialism. They all, however, rejected Marxism as overly deterministic and as 'unscientific' in its explanation of value. The progressivism of their thought helped to dampen any latent tendencies toward a revolutionary Marxism and to move the Swedish economy toward a model of democratic social engineering.

Contributors

Timothy Alborn, Department of the History of Science, Harvard University, Cambridge, Massachusetts

Louis Baeck, Centre for Development Planning, Katholicke Universiteit Leuven, Leuven, Belgium

William J. Barber, Department of Economics, Wesleyan University, Middletown, Connecticut

Mary Ann Dimand, Department of Economics, Glendon College, York University, Toronto, Ontario, Canada

Robert W. Dimand, Department of Economics, Brock University, St. Catharines, Ontario, Canada

Thomas M. Humphrey, Federal Reserve Bank of Richmond, Richmond, Virginia

Zoltan Kenessey, Senior Economist, Board of Governors of the Federal Reserve System, Washington, DC

André Lapidus, University of Paris – I, Paris, France

Johan Lönnroth, University of Göteborg, Göteborg, Sweden

S. Todd Lowry, Department of Economics, Washington and Lee University, Lexington, Virginia

Antoin Murphy, Department of Economics, Trinity College, Dublin, Ireland

John Vint, Department of Economics, Manchester Polytechnic, Manchester, England

PART 1

ASPECTS OF PRE-CLASSICAL ECONOMICS

1 The economic thought of classical Islam

Louis Baeck

The Mediterranean tradition

When asked for the date of birth of their science, most economists hesitate. Those who view the functioning of the economy as interrelated with the social and political matrix of the society at large – that is, who perceive it as political economy – trace its roots back to the Greek philosophers of antiquity. Some, with a macroeconomic inclination, would mention the mercantilists of the seventeenth century. Others would think of Adam Smith as the founding father of a 'classical' tradition. Those who take microeconomics as the hard core of economics might prefer the neoclassical triad consisting of Menger–Marshall–Walras. Still others would not care because in their view all predecessors of today's economic theory ought to be considered as prehistoric. To them ancient authors represent the underdeveloped stage of economics: one should not waste time reading past theories. This state of mind was characteristic of the post-war period. It brought the study of doctrinal history to a low ebb. This has recently been reversed.

In several European research centres a renewal of interest in the study of past doctrines is noticeable. Also new is the fact that researchers study them not solely out of historical interest. They are valued as sources of inspiration when attempting to solve actual problems on the intellectual level, especially by those researchers for whom mainstream economics offers no ready answer. One example is the revival of interest in the relationship between economics and ethics. In this vein, the Mediterranean tradition in economics offers fruitful inspiration. An important aspect of the Mediterranean tradition is its organicist and teleological perspective on society. In keeping with this focus, the economy is seen as subordinated to, and entangled in a complex web of social and political relations, ordered by ethical standards and norms. The Mediterranean tradition in economics started with Aristotle's text, *Ethica Nicomachea*, book V, chapter 5 and *Politica* book I, chapters 8–11.

In its development the Mediterranean tradition in economics was enriched by biblical thought, by the principles of Roman and Canonical law and, last but not least, by the Islamic and Christian scholastics (Baeck, 1987). In the sixteenth and seventeenth centuries, after more than two thousand years of hegemony in the material as well as in the intellectual field, the Mediterranean civilizations had lost their spell and relinquished their hold on history. The new nations of the North entered the scene and took over the initiative. In the wake of this 'Atlantization' a new, more disentangled conception of the economy blossomed.

In most reference works, the contribution of Islam has been left undiscussed. Even the standard work by Schumpeter, which treats the contribution of Greek antiquity and of the Christian scholastic period in some detail, mentions the name of Ibn Khaldoun only once (Schumpeter, 1954). The book of M. Grice-Hutchinson, the specialist in Spanish economic thought as well as the collection edited by S. Todd Lowry, with a valuable contribution on Islamic thought by M. Essid and T. Kuran, are on this point an exception to the rule (Grice-Hutchinson, 1978; Lowry, 1987).

The original source material regarding the economic thought of the Moslem world during its Golden Age (the period 750–1250) lies scattered over a large number of documents, some written in Persian and most in Arabic. The great majority of the commentaries on these documents have been produced by Western specialists in the field of oriental studies who, because of their philological background, have shown only little interest in the economic ideas contained in the texts they analysed. In the publications of the famous oriental-ist, G. von Grünebaum, not one single reference is made to the economic analysis formulated in that period (von Grünebaum, 1969; 1970). The second-ary literature is also scattered and scarce[1]. All this cools many a researcher's enthusiasm for embarking on this field of study.

In the historical unfolding of ideas, Islam's contribution to economic thought is more than simply a link in the transmission of classical culture to Europe. Islamic economic writings offer more than Greek texts in Arabic dress. They produced original ideas that have an innate value that cannot be found in the Greek sources.

Islam as a force in history

At the beginning of the seventh century, an inspired caravan merchant named Mohammed gave birth to a spiritual and social revolution in Arabia. This can be regarded as the last religious 'revelation' of antiquity. Islam was a religious and social response to the crisis in the clan society of Arabia. In Islam, the eroded social fabric of the clan was filled in with a binding element of a higher order: the *umma*, that is, the community of believers in Allah. The new religion stood in opposition to the latent polytheism of the Christian world (the doctrine of the Trinity, the veneration of the saints) as well as to the cosmic dualism of Persia. Allah was perceived as one and indivisible.

In the space of barely one century, Islam, driven by a holy zeal for Allah, would conquer an area stretching from Persia to Morocco and up to the Pyrenees in Europe. The first conquests of the Arabs were made in lands which had been the home of urban civilizations for thousands of years: that is, the river valleys of the Nile and the Tigris–Euphrates. With the conquest of the old centres of culture, Syria, Egypt and Persia, the new religion went through a process of spiritual, cultural and political deepening. Through this 'Iranization', the less developed conquerors absorbed the cultural legacy of the Sassanids, who centuries before had assimilated the Hellenic culture brought to them by Alexander. A magnificent civilization developed, centred first in Damascus, followed by Baghdad, and with a Western centre in Al-Andalus. From 750 to 1250 Islam was the hegemonic political and cultural power in the Mediterranean.

In the Eastern Empire and in the south of Spain (Cordoba) certain thinkers, notably Al-Farabi, Al-Ghazali, Al-Kindi, Ibn-Sina (Avicennes) and Ibn-Rushd (Averroës), experimented with Greek philosophy. It was through this link, incidentally, that the thought of Plato and Aristotle, on the basis of translations from Syriac and Arabic, broke through into the Latin West.

Islamic social order and religious inspiration rest on the message revealed through Mohammed which is contained in the Koran. The social and economic guidelines formulated in it are ethical in nature, that is, they are exhortations, commandments and prohibitions. Like those of the Jewish Bible and the Christian Gospels, however, they occasioned divergent interpretations by the intellectual establishment, especially by jurists, theologians and philosophers.

Three *suras* from the Koran deserve special attention[2].

1. The first prescript illustrates the social vision which comes to expression in the Koran. It relates to the so-called *zakat* tax, levied for the benefit of the poor. Apart from the specific indication of those it is meant to benefit (the Moslem at the bottom of the economic scale), the text of the Koran remains vague. From the context it is very clear that it is a matter of a tax levied not only on income, but also on property. Thus the very well-to-do must, in fairness, make the greatest contribution. We are left in the dark as to whether within the Islamic community other taxes may also be levied. During the development of Moslem society into a complex urban civilization, this question would lead to divergent views between the modernists and the traditionalists or fundamentalists. In fact, the taxes for financing general public spending were originally levied on the groups in the population that did not belong to the *umma*: that is, on the Jews and the Christians.

2. A second injunction relates to the prohibition of *riba* (financial interest) which was regarded as usury. On this point the Koran accords with the view held in antiquity that money is a neutral instrument of exchange, which in itself cannot create any surplus value[3]. The biblical texts of

Deuteronomy, Ezekiel and the Gospel of Luke contain similar injunctions against usury.

Although the *riba* prohibition in the text of the Koran refers to the interest calculated on credit loans for basic necessities such as food, this passage was interpreted in a later period as a prohibition of any interest taking. This rule also led to divergent viewpoints between modernists and fundamentalists. It may seem paradoxical that in Islamic teaching the *riba* prohibition was instituted by Mohammed, who was himself more acquainted with trade and finance than Aristotle and the later Christian church fathers. While the latter, after a centuries-long scholastic debate, morally legitimized the charging of financial interest, *riba* in Islamic teaching has remained up to the present a moral stumbling block to the development of the banking system (Siddiqi, 1981).

3.   The third specific commandment relates to inheritance law. Although the Koran recognizes the right of private ownership, the free disposition of an estate by bequest is limited. Bequeathing an estate to the advantage of a single recipient is regarded as conflicting with the general social views of the Islamic community. Only one-third can be distributed by free choice in the will. For the remaining two-thirds, the Koran prescribes the distribution of the inheritance according to a formula regulated by custom. These verses of the Koran have put a brake on the accumulation of wealth through the fragmentation which results from the customary distribution of the inheritance.

It is clear from the above-mentioned commandments that the Koran presents specific norms in a few areas, but that the text, being a moral and religious revelation, contains no comprehensive economic doctrine. The same can be said of the Jewish Bible and of the Christian Gospels. The difference, however, is that for more than three centuries the Galilean message had the status of a minority religion in the Roman Empire. As such it had no responsibility for the economic organization of the Empire. Moreover, when Emperor Constantine installed Christianity as the official religion of the Empire, the western part, exhausted by the pressure from the barbarians, went into decline. The urban economy lapsed into stagnation and was replaced by the subsistence economy of the large estates. During the thousand years of rural slumber which followed in the West, the Roman Church was able to get along with a few simple commandments.

Islam followed a different historical course. Through the rapid conquest of an extensive Empire, with an intense flow of trade among its great cities, the young religion was confronted with the challenge of coming up with a more complete economic doctrine than that contained in the Koran. The complexity of its urban conquests impelled Islam to an immediate creativity regarding concepts and doctrines of political, social and economic organization. In working this out, the thinkers and leaders of the *umma* in the golden age would draw their inspiration from the Persian cultural legacy and from the Greek philosophers.

The economic thought of the golden age

The 'mirror for princes' literature

With the conquest of Persia, followed by the establishment of the ruling dynasty of the Abbasids in Baghdad, the Islamic conquerors were confronted with a more highly developed culture and with an oriental (authoritarian) administration. The Iranization of Islam inevitably brought in its wake a greater depth of doctrine relating to economic problems. Thus a symbiosis was achieved between the socio-economic commandments contained in the Koran and the ideas offered by Persian culture in this field.

This symbiosis found its literary expression in the writings of scholars and viziers who, in the name of the public interest, presented an ideal of just and efficient government to the rulers. These open letters are known as 'mirrors for princes' literature or mirror-books (Richter, 1932; Sourdel, 1959; Dawood, 1965; Lambton, 1971; Grice-Hutchinson, 1978; Essid, 1988).

An impressive group of authors expressed themselves in this genre: Al-Dimashqi (a writer from the ninth century), Al-Farabi (887–950), Al-Biruni (975–1056), Al-Ghazali (1058–1111) and Al-Turtushi (1059–1126). Here we are mentioning only the most influential (Laoust, 1970).

The mirror-books abound in discussions of public administration, the fiscal system, the efficient organization of commerce, and just government. The last is held up as an ideal before the prince. In his discussion, Al-Farabi refers to the economic ideas contained in the works of Plato and Aristotle. The philosopher Al-Ghazali limited himself to a more orthodox Moslem tradition (Ghazanfar and Islahi, 1988). After a journey to India, Al-Biruni presented the example of the Indian princes to the sultan. Al-Dimashqi, the most economic thinker of them all, even formulated what modern economists would call a price theory (Bousquet, 1957). In this theory, he makes a distinction between normal periods in which market prices are based on cost of production, and periods of scarcity or oversupply, in which the speculative drive manifests itself. Al-Dimashqi's work is in fact a didactic handbook of commerce in which he sketches the ideal merchant and his social role in contributing to the common good of the community (Desomogyi, 1965). The merchant is the link between supply and demand in the market, or between parties who have, respectively, a surplus (supply) or deficit (demand) in certain products. The social function becomes optimal when the merchant manages to refrain from speculative profiteering, as well as from the urge to accumulate riches. Al-Dimashqi does, however, regard a normal profit as being the fair wage of a merchant.

In an entertaining style, full of anecdotes, Al-Dimashqi offers a coherent and complete formulation of the market mechanism. Moreover he clearly sympathizes with the merchant. In a notable passage he cites a Persian author, Ash-Shaybani, who in his book *Kitab al Kash* (or the Book of Merits) professes that making money as a merchant is of greater value for the community than earning an income as a bureaucrat or in the military. Al-Dimashqi's work was clearly written as a plea for the benefit of the merchant class, which formed an up-and-coming and influential group in the Abbasid empire. This was a development which the fundamentalists looked upon with scorn (Ritter, 1917). Most mirror authors proclaim the ethic of the golden mean, in which the exaggerated urge to accumulate and the speculative impulse are condemned. Equity is heralded as the supreme norm of an efficient public administration and of a just economic order.

The organization of the city and of the household

A second source of economic views is the literature on the *tadbir al-madina*, the organization of the city, and about the *tadbir al-manzil*, the organization of the household. The latter texts contain detailed discussions on the structuring of the family economy and on the respective roles of the head of the family, the women, the children, the slaves. These texts offer, above all, an insight into the most important cell of the society. As such, they form interesting study material from a microeconomic standpoint.

The literature on the *tadbir al-madina* is important for the study of evolving economic thought in Islam. Some writings provide penetrating analyses of market activity in the urban centres of the Islamic world. Each city had one or even several market sheriffs who were supposed to keep watch over commercial transactions. The sheriff carried the title of *sahib al-suk* or, literally, master of the merchants' guild. His responsibility was to make sure that markets functioned in a fair and orderly way. Above the market sheriff was the head of the commercial court, who was called *muhtasib*. He worked in close contact with the religious authorities. His functions and fields of action are described with great detail in the literature (Lewis, 1937; Marçais, 1954; Sherwani, 1956; Chalmeta, 1973; Al-Raziq, 1979; Islahi, 1985).

The primeval economic thought in Islam remains embedded in the religious, moral and political framework as presented in the Koran. The literature on the *tadbir al-madina*, however, differs from the mirror literature, since the former was produced by jurists and civil servants who wrote on the basis of their experience as market sheriffs or chairmen of the commercial court and who thereby completed and made explicit the simple norms contained in the Koran.

In these abundant and at times tedious texts, the careful reader occasionally comes across flashes of economic insight into the market mechanism.

It is not possible to give a complete overview of the jurisprudential traditions (*hisbah* literature) which thus developed. Its volume is enormous. Also, different traditions developed in the various cities of the Islamic world: Baghdad, Cairo, Kairouan, Damascus, Cordoba, etc. To a certain extent, economic thought is a product of concrete circumstances. The great cities of the Moslem world formed urban centres with great concentrations of population, surrounded by relatively underdeveloped rural communities and Bedouin settlements. Supply for the urban centres was a permanent problem which became more acute in times of harvest failure or natural disasters such as floods or, by contrast, of extreme drought. In view of this situation, it was to be expected that the perspective of analyses in commercial and economic thought would concentrate on the market mechanism.

In the Koran itself, Mohammed is a proponent of the free market. But the complexity and fragility of the urban supply lines occasioned price fluctuations. These encouraged the religious and administrative authorities to control and regulate the free market. The *muhtasib* played a central role in the supervision of the market. It was his duty to keep watch over the upward drift of prices, as well as over weights, measures and over the money exchange rates in the financial markets. Any price rises were seen by the urban poor as being the result of manipulation by greedy merchants hungry for speculative profits. From the point of view of the central authorities, the *muhtasib* had not only a religious and economic supervisory function. He also fulfilled a social and political role, in that he kept social protest – or revolt – under control in times of scarcity and famine.

From the standpoint of economic doctrine, the writings of Ibn Taymiya deserve our attention[4]. More than his *muhtasib* colleagues, he carried out a theoretical analysis of the market mechanism and his discourses on the advantages and disadvantages of regulation and deregulation have an almost contemporary ring to us (Laoust, 1939; Ahmad, 1961).

His work contains a detailed description of the law of supply and demand. In his analysis of the supply side, the author makes an important distinction between local production and supply from abroad through imports. Moreover, he discusses their respective price elasticities. In the study of the demand side, he mentions the important determinants of demand, such as the number and the purchasing power of the (potential) buyers, the situation of scarcity or abundance in the market, the socio-psychological condition of the buyers, and the assessment of their utility (indifference) function. The factors of prestige and status play a considerable role in the trade in luxuries. We can consider Ibn Taymiya to be a medieval forerunner of the Veblenian theory of 'conspicuous consumption'.

In fact he very nearly reaches a symbiosis of the later developments between the objective and subjective theories of value. In a normal market, merchants and artisans ask for the coverage of their cost price plus a surplus for their risk. This is a loose version of the present day mark-up theory. In a more speculative market situation, (i.e., one dominated by scarcity or, in contrast, by abundance), the subjective evaluations of the market participants play an important role. His description and analyses are based on concrete observations of market activity. In his function as *muhtasib*, writes Ibn Taymiya, he acquired much practical experience as to the manner in which surplus value originates, for example, in the processing of raw materials by artisans, or with merchants, money changers, renters of public baths, etc.

In the debate between the supporters of the free market as presented in the Koran and the proponents of official price setting by the central administration, Ibn Taymiya opts for an intermediate position. In fact he is an advocate of an *ad hoc* market regulation on the basis of concrete situations. Occasional intervention by the central authorities may be helpful to assure the fulfilment of the basic needs of the people. Thus he is a proponent of control for the purpose of curbing speculative peaks, but he rejects general price setting by market guilds or by the authorities as being inefficient.

In Ibn Taymiya's lifetime the debasement of money became a frequent practice which was frowned upon by the Muslim jurists since it was contrary to the community ethics. The merchants and the people deplored this state of affairs but could only mutter their misgivings against this public fraud. Ibn Taymiya analyses the monetary development of his time in the lucid way of a privileged observer. His treatment of money is more sociological than that of Averroës, the philosopher, who preceded him by hundred and fifty years and who reasoned along more abstract, Aristotelian lines. A generation later than the *muhtasib* from Cairo, Nicholas Oresme would write his treatise in the same vein.

The philosophical tradition of Ibn Rushd

In its expansion into the old cultural lands of the East (Syria, Persia), Islam came into contact with Greek philosophy and with the Persian intellectual tradition. The Greeks had reflected on cosmology, ethics, politics and also economy from the point of view of the natural order. Islam's world view was anchored in the supernatural order. As such it became the third religion of the Mediterranean based on a revealed book (Bible, Gospel, Koran). On the way eastward, the new religion as expressed in Islamic theology (*kalam*) was confronted with Greek rationalism.

These were two different worlds of thought. The scene was clearly set for a major dispute between the more traditional *ulama*, the philosophers and the theologians. This dispute raged from the tenth to the twelfth centuries. Al-

Ghazali systematically set out to dismantle the philosophical edifice constructed by Avicennes. Some of the great theologians and philosophers of the Mediterranean cultures endeavoured to reconcile the two in a scholastic synthesis[5]. The *ulama* and the theologians insisted on perfection in morals; however, the philosophers insisted on perfection in knowledge and understanding as well. In this the scholars of Islam preceded the Jewish and Christian scholastics who, on this point, learned much from their forerunners.

In the first period of bloom, Al-Farabi, Al-Ghazali and Ibn Sina are the major figures to be noted. They lived and wrote in the cities of eastern Islam such as Baghdad, Cairo and Damascus. They were familiar with the work of the Pythagoreans, Plato and Aristotle. But their conceptual world, that is, the supernatural conception of cosmic and human events, was closer to that of Neoplatonism. Within the context of Neoplatonic thought the philosopher is regarded as a seeker of contact with the world of ideas and spiritual forms as a prerequisite of union with God.

Ibn Rushd (Averroës 1126–98), a philosopher of western Islam, took Aristotle as his master (Peters, 1968; Badawi, 1988). Some later writers called him the father of Islamic rationalism. This brought him into disrepute with the fundamentalists who frowned upon his rationalism as opium for the pious Moslem. Averroës lived and worked in Sevilla and later in Cordoba, the splendid capital of Al-Andalus. But at one time he had to flee to North Africa on account of his Greek heresies. Averroës was a universal mind who mastered brilliantly the science and knowledge of his time. One of the great texts by Averroës is his treatise on the harmony of religion and philosophy. In this work the relationship between the revealed ethics of the Koran and the ethical norms based on independent reasoning is examined.

One important issue in the 'reason/revelation' controversies was the question whether an action is right because God says it is right, or whether God says it is right because it is right. Averroës argues for the objectivity of ethics as opposed to the subjectivism which had become orthodox in Islam. Given his belief in a divinely revealed law (*sharia*) he proclaims that there are parts of the *sharia* which are to be accepted without question. He also studied questions of practical ethics, that is, politics and political economy, but he did not produce much in the realm of economic theory. The little he wrote, however, was of great importance because of its later influence on the Christian scholastics, especially those who are considered to be of the Averroist school (Grabmann, 1931; Gauthier, 1947; Actes, 1978; Langholm, 1979).

Averroës produced commentaries on two important socio-economic texts, the *Republic* of Plato and the Nicomachean *Ethics* of Aristotle. For an evaluation of his text on the *Republic*, the reader is referred to the literature (Rosenthal, 1965; Buttenwurth, 1975). It is remarkable that Averroës gives more attention to the ideas of Plato on the guided democracy than to the political theories formulated by Aristotle. Averroës lived in a time of political turmoil with weak, opportunistic emirs. The ideal of a strong 'philosopher–king' may very well have appealed to him.

His commentary on the Nicomachean *Ethics* of Aristotle is more important for our argument[6]. For the Stagirite, ethics is applied philosophy, that is, ethics has to do with the practical ordering of human existence[7]. The end of human beings is happiness in accordance with moral virtue and practical wisdom. In a well ordered city-state, human endeavours are directed to *eudaimonia*, to the harmonious, good life. The economy and its ordering of material welfare can help realize this but the organization of the economy cannot be a goal. It is only a means to achieve well-being. This last is a category of a higher order. The good life can only be realized in the city-state, where man lives in a societal context.

For Aristotle economics is 'political' economy. In Aristotle's economic world, equity (an ethical norm) has priority over optimization of the growth rate or the capacity to accumulate wealth. The Aristotelian model not only sets external limits to growth (resources) but also internal ones (Lowry, 1987). The ethical norm of the just mean puts a bridle on the desire to accumulate. Averroës adopts this hierarchical ordering between economics, politics and ethics. He adds to this that the revealed truth in the Koran also subordinates economics to the revealed ethics of the supernatural order.

The reading and interpretation of Averroës' commentary on the Nicomachean *Ethics* presents a problem because the original Arabic text no longer exists. It is thus a matter of working with a Latin version that was often cited by the Christian scholastics and which therefore has been preserved[8]. In 1240 in the translation centre in Toledo, Averroës' commentary was put into Latin by Hermannus Alemannus, with the title *Liber Nicomachiae*. Different versions of it came into circulation in the Christian West. According to specialists, the most reliable edition is that of Leonardo Bruni of Arezzo, who was called Aretus[9]. His text was printed in 1489 in Venice. This edition presents both versions, that of Hermannus Alemannus as well as the philologically purged version of Aretus. With the exception of C. Miller and M. Grice-Hutchinson, Averroës' commentary has, to my knowledge, remained undiscussed by the historians of economic doctrine (Miller, 1925; Grice-Hutchinson, 1978).

Whoever compares the original version of Aristotle with Averroës' commentary will be struck by the harmony of thought between the two philosophers in the realm of economics. On one important point Averroës parts company with Aristotle: in the theory of money. First and most importantly, the Arabian scholar brings more clarity into the Stagirite's somewhat confusing formulation. This has already caused a lot of headaches for many an analyst. Averroës introduces a correction into the nominalistic view of money. In a clear style, the three functions of money are described and analysed: as a means of exchange, a measure of value for all other goods and services (*metron* in Greek, *mensura* in Latin) and as a store of value for transactions in the future (in the text, 'tangulam fidejussor supplendi necessitatem futuram'). Aristotle had clearly recognized the functions of money as a means of exchange and measure of value; but his view of its function as a reserve of liquidity remained somewhat vague. It was Averroës who clearly saw money in its function as 'reserve' buying power.

This brings us to a second remark in connection with the essence of money. Is money, among other things, also a commodity, like any other, which without problem may change in value through an 'official' revaluation as well as through fluctuations in supply and demand (cf. the quantity theory)? Or does it constitute a 'genus' apart because of its essential functions? These questions were not clearly sorted out by Aristotle.

The Stagirite emerges as a monetary nominalist, that is, he perceives the value of money as a value set by socio-political convention (*nomos* in Greek) and from this comes the term *numisma* for money. In this way the community can, at its own discretion, regulate its value by means of currency adjustment. Averroës lived in a different cultural and religious world, in which for various reasons any change in value of money appeared unacceptable to him. First of all, there is the philosophical argument: a standard of value cannot be conceived to be changeable, because otherwise social and economic relations end up in arbitrariness and indetermination. Allah, as the measure of all things, is unchangeable. All essential measurements, such as the value of the dinar and the dirham, are subject to this law. There is, additionally, the argument of social equity and fairness. If money is a reserve for future purchasing power, then changing its value constitutes an unfair arbitrariness. Revaluation means a pure monetary profit and is equal to usury (*riba*). By a devaluation of the monetary standard people are bereft of part of their reserve of liquidity or capital.

In his study of Averroës' *Commentary*, Rosenthal maintained that the Arabic scholar professed a monetary nominalism in the Aristotelean sense[10]. It seems to me that this exegesis presents a problem. In the first place, it seems irreconcilable with the philosophical and cultural context in which Averroës thought and wrote. Further, in the mentioned version of Aretus, there is no textual support to be found for such a classification. In the passage in which Aristotle sets in perspective the possibility of a change in value for money, one reads in Averroës' commentary the following: 'Et quum ista inveniatur in denario expone ut sit nomen legis apud grecos denominative sumptum a positione, nominatus est denarius in lingua greca nomine denominative sumpto a lege'. This passage is simply a confirmation from Averroës that the Greeks and Aristotle held a nominalistic view, which in their society could be confirmed by the law.

The Averroïsts in the Latin scholastic period developed Averroës' line of thought about the unchangeability of money as a standard. In the scholastic period after Thomas Aquinus, both Oresme and Buridanus wrote against the 'corruptio' of money, that is, against the kind of currency fraud practised by the rulers of their time.

The crisis literature

By the second half of the thirteenth century the Golden Age of Islam was past. The *umma* was in a state of strife and social disruption. Persia was conquered by the Seldjuks, followed by the advance of the Moghuls out of Asia. In Egypt the Mameluks ruled. And in Spain the *reconquista* of the Catholic princes of Aragon, Castille, Navarra and Asturia was pressing the Moslems onto the defensive. The consequences were loss of territory and intensification of internal disputes. The *Sitz im Leben* of thought, including economic thought, was thus one of decline.

The Persian author Nasir al-Din Tusi (1201–74), an advisor to the rising Moghul Hulalu, wrote a work about public finance and monetary questions. He relied heavily on the Greek Pythagorean Bryson (Plessner, 1928). On the technical level, Tusi's handbook does not contain many new insights. It is characteristic that the author argued in favour of the 'Islamicization' of the economic system, with a stricter application of the Islamic tradition in public affairs. For the period in which decline set in, the following authors are of importance: Ibn Khaldoun (1332–1406), Al-Maqrizi (1364–1442), and to a lesser degree Al-Dawani (1427–1501). The first two are historians of fame, who direct their attention to 'developmental problems'. They attribute the decline of Islamic civilization to the unsound social and economic policies of the rulers. Unsound in their context is not only a technical concept, it is also a moral category.

The global vision of Ibn Khaldoun

Ibn Khaldoun was born in Tunis in the year 1332 to an aristocratic Moorish–Andalusian family. In 1242 the Catholic princes had conquered the city of Seville and the surrounding region, so that the Islamic lands in Spain were limited to the emirate of Granada. The Khaldoun family had subsequently emigrated to North Africa. Ibn Khaldoun led a busy life as a higher-level civil servant, jurist and historian. His master work is a global vision of the historical development of societies, with the title *Kitab al-ibar*. The long introduction, or *Muqadimmah*, is a synthesis of his theory on socio-economic evolution. F. Rosenthal produced à translation of the work and N. Dawood published an abridged version (Dawood, 1967). Although he got little response from his contemporaries, Ibn Khaldoun has recently attracted more attention in the West than any of the other Islamic authors. The secondary literature is impressive

(Mahmasani, 1932; Qadir, 1942; Spengler, 1963; Andic, 1965; Nassar, 1967; Lacoste, 1969; Sherwani, 1970; Syed, 1970; Boulakia, 1971).

Ibn Khaldoun was the first Arabic author to produce a global picture of the economy. He analysed the production process, formulated a theory of distribution and studied the influence of public financing on both. Khaldoun was very conscious of the cyclical character of economic phenomena. His price and value theory is based on labour costs but is scantier than the more nuanced analysis of Ibn Taymiya. His demographic analysis is original and pioneering. Central to his theory is the idea of group cohesion (*asabiah*) as the motor of welfare or, in its absence, of decline. According to him, tribal cohesion is strongest in Bedouin society, but in the cities, *asabiah* progressively weakens. This inevitably leads to decline. The cycle of socio-economic regeneration is then only possible when new dynasties, supported by the Bedouins with their healthy community spirit, conquer the decadent cities and begin a new cycle.

In the *Muqadimmah*, a piece of work which was ahead of its time, Ibn Khaldoun probes the social, economic and institutional factors which influence history. He can be labelled as a political scientist, a sociologist and an economist. Some make him out to be a Marxist economist. In my view, this is going too far because, on the one hand, Ibn Khaldoun invokes the social solidarity, religious conviction and political power – or the decline of political power – as explanations of economic phenomena; on the other hand, he clearly opts for a market economy.

Besides the theoretical analysis, part five of the *Muqadimmah* contains a detailed description of the different professions of that time. The theoretical part refers constantly to the Koran and shows an affinity with the conceptions of Al-Dimashqi. Nevertheless it contains various innovative concepts which are brought together in a coherent, dynamic system.

In the first place, there is the theory of production. Production, according to Ibn Khaldoun, is a human activity which is organized socially and internationally. Man produces in order to be able to provide for his necessities and in this he makes use of his labour, which is at the same time the most important factor in production. Because man as an individual cannot himself provide for all his needs, specialization and division of labour come into being in social co-operation. The result of this is, however, that on an individual level more is produced than is necessary for survival. The surplus thus produced can be traded. He regards the value of each product as equal to the amount of work put into it. Therefore it is not the dimension (volume) of the currency reserve which measures the prosperity of a country, but the degree of specialization among its inhabitants. The reason for this is that a greater specialization or division of labour results in greater production, a larger surplus to be traded and thus higher profit and more prosperity. Ibn Khaldoun's monetary conceptions are extremely primitive. He regards gold and silver as the two natural, God-created forms of money. According to him a religious institution should be responsible for controlling the weights of the coins and their value. The prices of gold and silver should not change. They are the standards of value. The prices of all other goods and services may, however, fluctuate according to market conditions.

With his theory of distribution, Ibn Khaldoun approached in an intuitive manner some national accounting concepts. He saw the price of a product as being composed of three elements: compensation for the producer (wages), compensation for the merchant (profit) and compensation for the authorities (tax). He recognized that the payment for each of these three elements is influenced by the demand for and the supply of the products in question. On the one hand, supply and demand are determined by the number of producers and consumers, for example, by the size of the population and their will to produce and to consume. On the other hand, supply and demand conditions are also influenced by the tax policies of the government. These two determining factors are, according to Ibn Khaldoun, subject to a cyclical movement.

Regarding population, he reasoned as follows: the more people there are, the greater the specialization that is possible and the greater the prosperity. This great prosperity allows the growth of the population, which in turn stimulates the process of specialization and accumulation. Richer regions see their cities grow and become more prosperous, and the poor get poorer. The cumulative growth process cannot, however, go on without problems, because urban migration will provoke two insoluble bottlenecks. First, cities grow too large and decline sets in. Second, the flight from rural areas brings about a decrease in agricultural production. The results are famine and disease and, ultimately, a decrease in the population.

With regard to the national budget, Ibn Khaldoun outlined the following cyclical movement. Originally the power of the state is limited, the rate of taxation is at a low level, and fiscal proceeds are small. This stimulates the will to consume and produce but rising production brings with it a growing tax revenue for the government. In this way, the power of the state is strengthened. This results in a rise in the tax rate, which causes government revenues to rise even more. Ultimately the tax rate reaches such a high level that it leads to a fall in production and consumption. This reduces the aggregate state revenues and affects the power of the state. Ibn Khaldoun maintained that, at some point in this process, an optimal relationship will exist between the volume of income production and the level of taxation. If this level of taxation is exceeded through the fiscal exactions of the ruler, sooner or later the social fabric will break and will be brought to the brink of revolution. Rulers who proceed to excessive tax pressure break the norms of well-ordered government, with the result that a vicious spiral of fraud and tax evasion sets in.

Ibn Khaldoun formulated the advantages of the division of labour long before Adam Smith, he invented a population cycle theory before Malthus and in terms of fiscal economy he formulated ideas which are comparable with those of supply side economics. The *Muqadimmah*, as well as the complete text of the *Kitab al-ibar*, is well written and enjoyable. It constitutes a strong and balanced argument addressed to the rulers and other influential persons of its time. The text aims at a renewed community spirit and efficient government to give Islam a new developmental impulse. Ibn Khaldoun reminds his contemporaries of Islam's splendid past achievements and becomes nostalgic about its decline which, with a sharp mind, he analyses. During his lifetime, however, he had no success with his message.

Al-Maqrizi

Al-Maqrizi held the position of *muhtasib* in Cairo under the dynasty of the Mameluks. He left behind a large body of work, of which only two studies are of importance for the history of economic doctrines: a 'Study of the Famines' and a 'Study of the Monetary System'. Although Al-Maqrizi opens up interesting perspectives on the economic problems of his time, he has only recently been 'rediscovered' (Minost, 1936; Oulalou, 1976; Hennequin, 1979). The analysis of Al-Maqrizi, more than that of Ibn Khaldoun, is an investigation of the causes of the 'system crisis' in the economy of his time.

Scarcity and famine, according to him, are the result not only of natural disasters such as the fact that the Nile in certain periods brings too much irrigation water and in other periods too little. A problem created by a natural factor can always be solved through human organization. In the Golden Age of Islam, and even in the time of the great Pharaohs, there was little or no problem with the Nile. Al-Maqrizi sought the cause of the crisis in the socio-economic failures of the regime. The country was saddled with a feudal class which skimmed off surplus production by excessive taxation and oppressive corvées. The second means of skimming off the income (buying power) is situated in the monetary sector. In Egypt there were three types of coin in circulation: the golden *di*nar, the silver *dirham* and the copper *fals* (plural *foulous*).

In order to fill the national treasury, the rulers of the Mameluk dynasty put more and more of the lower-valued *foulous* in circulation. In fact, this was a disguised devaluation (currency fraud). To protect themselves, the wealthy classes began hoarding the more valuable dinar and dirham. In later economic literature, this substitution would become known under the name of 'Gresham's Law'. In contrast with Gresham, who only formulated this substitution (bad currency drives out good), Al-Maqrizi went deeper into the mechanism of substitution. In his explanation he goes beyond the mere monetary dimension of the crisis by situating it in the global religious and social context.

He saw the debasement of money as a symptom of a general crisis in values. The rule of the Mameluks, rife with corruption in public administration, had become socially inefficient. Al-Maqrizi formulates it thus: the inefficient administration drove out the good. The feudal top classes were squeezing out the masses. The fair distribution of burdens and duties had given way to fraudulent rule, with a disregard of the guidelines contained in the Koran.

As a Moslem economist, Al-Maqrizi associates money as a standard of value (*namus al-adil*) with the law of the Almighty, the *namus al-Akbar*. The monetary system can be reorganized only if the overall socio-economic and political system is put in order, that is, by applying the guidelines contained in the Koran. With religious zeal he wrote, 'Almighty, inspire our sultan to apply himself to the recovery of our *umma* so that the dirham once again will become the standard of value for all other (also foreign) currencies, just as Allah is the absolute standard of value for both the governors and the governed'. The inflation of prices caused by currency manipulation was for Al-Maqrizi not only a monetary phenomenon. For him, a sick currency is the product of a (morally) sick society.

In conclusion we also mention Al-Dawani (1427–1501), a Persian author who leaned strongly towards the analyses of Tusi and Al-Maqrizi. He can be regarded as a vulgarizer who comes up with no new insights. Like Maqrizi, he clearly comes out as an Islamic economist by maintaining that fair and efficient government is only possible if the authorities keep the currency inviolable as the measuring rod of goods and services. As a step in this direction, he suggested placing the monetary system under the control of the highest religious authority, the caliphate.

Conclusion
Economic thought is a product of the society in which it is rooted and is thus culturally determined. It is a product of its time. The Greek philosophers saw the population and the economy of the *polis* as the material foundation subordinated to the socio-political fabric. The societal relationships and especially the political order belonged to the higher category of the formal structure. For them, the socio-political structure determined the constituting element of the society. Plato and Aristotle praised the Greek polis, with its community bonds determined by ethical norms, as the supreme form of human society.

Only in this social cohesion could man develop in a full and balanced way, and live the good life. Individual accumulation (*krematistikè*) and that of the family (the *oikos*) was subordinate to the solidarity of the social fabric. The desire to accumulate might lead to social disruption. Economics, in this vision, was 'political' economy. It was guided by the ethic of the golden mean; it was *oikos-nomos*.

Islam took over this organicist and teleological tradition of thought and enriched the Greek ethic of the natural order with the transcendental injunctions of the Koran. This synthesis was later enriched in the Christian scholastic period of the late Middle Ages. Islam thus formed an essential link in the

Mediterranean tradition of economic thought. This came to an end with the Spanish scholastic period of the sixteenth century. After this two-thousand-year hegemony of the Mediterranean tradition, the torch was passed to the scholars of the emerging Atlantic nations. In the Atlantic tradition, the economic aspect will come to be detached from the social and political aspects in which it is embedded and become a goal in itself. It develops toward a 'pure' economics.

Compared to the concepts of the Greek pioneers, the contribution of Islam to economic theory signifies a remarkable broadening and deepening of thought. The Islamic civilizations were less biased against trading and money matters than the Greek philosophers and the Christian scholastics. They did, however, formulate strict ethical norms in application to production, distribution and exchange, as well as to public finance and the monetary system. They laid particular stress on the moral inviolability of the standards. In the specific domain of monetary economy, the Islamic authors produced pioneer work which goes beyond Aristotelian nominalism and corrects it. Currency manipulation or excessive taxation were impermissible in their eyes because, ethically and socially, they constitute unfair manipulation and abuse of power.

In our world with its fluctuating exchange rates and unstable norms, the analyses of the Islamic authors offer a resourceful inspiration for more stability in value standards and currencies.

Notes

1. The King Abdulaziz University of Jeddah created in 1976 an International Centre for Research in Islamic Economics. Since 1981 the Centre has published research papers on the history of economic thought in Islam. In Pakistan there is also a revival of study in the history of Islamic economic thought.
2. Sura: one of the 124 chapters of the Koran.
3. In the economic texts of Aristotle, pure financial profit (interest) is dealt with as *krematistikè*, that is, as unnatural and objectionable accumulation. Aristotle also proclaimed that money does not breed. The Latin scholastic, Albertus Magnus, formulated this principle in his flamboyant manner: 'Pecunia non parit'.
4. Ibn Taymiya (1262–1328) lived in Cairo and belonged to the Hanbalite sect. His time was one of intense sectional and religious strife. He was a prominent scholar and prolific writer. Some modern reform movements in Islam draw on Ibn Taymiya's work as a source of inspiration. In the research centres of contemporary Islamic economics, especially Lahore and Jeddah, his economic texts have been analysed in some detail (Siddiqi, 1981 and 1982).
5. The interaction between *kalam* and philosophy has been studied in some detail. The synthesis of Anawati and Gardet offers a handsome introduction to this Islamic scholastic tradition (Anawati & Gardet, 1948) while the recent book of Leaman offers a philosopher's perspective (Leaman, 1985).
6. In his commentary on the *Nicomachean Ethics*, Averroës is indebted to Al-Farabi (Salman, 1939).
7. Stagirite: a native or inhabitant of Stagira, a city of ancient Macedonia; Aristotle was born there and was also called by Atheneans, the Stagirite.
8. There exists also a Hebrew version of Averroës' commentary (Berman, 1978).

9.   Under the auspices of the Medieval Academy of America a complete edition of the *Corpus Commentarum Averrois in Aristotelem*, was started years ago; it is still in progress.
10. According to Rosenthal, 'nomocracy' is the common basis of Greek and Islamic political philosophy. In a recent study, Berti stresses the 'common values' (Berti, 1988).

References

Actes du Colloque International sur Averroës, *Multiple Averroës*, ed. Les Belles Lettres, Paris, 1978.

Ahmad, I. (1961), 'Ibn Taymiya on Islamic Economics', *Voice of Islam*, **11**, August, pp. 557–69, Karachi.

Al-Raziq, A. (1979), 'La Hisba et le muhtasib en Egypte aux temps des Mammelouks', *Annales Islamologiques*, pp. 115–78, Paris.

Anawati, G. & Gardet, L. (1948), *Introduction à la théologie musulmane*, Paris, Vrin.

Andic, S. (1965), 'A Fourteenth Century Sociology of Public Finance', *Public Finance*, **20**, (1), pp. 22–44.

Badawi, A. (1988), 'Aristote le maître à penser du monde musulman' in M. Sinaceur (ed.), *Aristote Aujourd'hui*, Paris: Unesco, pp. 164–77.

Baeck, L. (1987), 'Aristotle as Mediterranean Economist', *Diogenes*, (138), pp. 81–104, Paris.

Berman, L. (1978), 'Ibn Rushd's Middle Commentary in the Nichomachean Ethics in Medieval Hebrew Literature', in *Multiple Averroës*, pp. 287–322, Paris.

Berti, E. (1988), 'L'idée aristotélicienne de société politique dans les traditions musulmane et juive' in Turcica, (ed.), *L'influence d'Aristote dans le monde méditerranéen*, Istanbul: ISIS, pp. 99–116.

Boulakia, J. (1971), 'Ibn Khaldoun: a Fourteenth Century Economist', *Journal of Political Economy*, **79**, Sept.–Oct., pp. 1105–18.

Bousquet, G. (1957), 'L'economie politique non-européano-chrétienne', *Revue d'Histoire Economique et Sociale*, **45**, pp. 5–23, Paris.

Buttenwurth, C. (1975), 'New Light on the Political Philosophy of Avenoes', in G.F. Hourani (ed.) *Essays on Islamic Philosophy and Science*, Paris, Albany: *State University of New York*.

Chalmeta, P. (1973), *El señor del Zoco en España*, pp. LXIX and 761, Madrid: Instituto Hispano-Arabe de Cultura.

Dawood, A. (1965). 'A Comparative Study of Arabic and Persian Mirrors from the Second to the Sixth Century after Hegira', Unpublished Study, University of London.

Dawood, N. (1967), *The Muqadimmah: an Introduction to History*, pp. XIV and 465, Princeton: Princeton University Press.

Desomogyi, J. (1965), 'Economic Theory in Classical Arabic Literature', *Studies in Islam*, **2**, January, pp. 1–6, Delhi.

Essid, M. (1987), 'Islamic Economic Thought', in S. Todd Lowry (ed.), *Pre-classical Economic Thought*, pp. 77–102, Boston: Kluwer.

Essid, M. (1988), 'Les Écrivains grecs et la genèse de la pensée économique, les développements médiévaux chez les auteurs arabes', unpublished Ph. D. thesis, Paris.

Gauthier, R. (1947), 'Trois commentaires averroïstes sur l'ethique à Nicomaque', in *Archives d'histoire doctrinale et littéraire du Moyen Age*, **16**, pp. 187–336.

Ghanzanfar, S. (1988), 'Scholastic Economics and Arab Scholars: the Great Gap Thesis Reconsidered', 15th Annual 1988 History of Economics Society Meetings, Toronto.

Ghazanfar, S. and Islahi, A. (1988), 'Economic Thought of an Arab Scholastic: Abu Hamid Al-Ghazali, 1058–1111', Unpublished paper, Jeddah.

Grabmann, M. (1931), *Der Lateinische Averroismus des 13. Jahrhunderts und seine Stellung zur christlichen Weltanschauung*, Munich: Sitzungsberichte der Bayerischen Akademie der Wissenschaft.

Grice-Hutchinson, M. (1978), *Early Economic Thought in Spain*, London: Allen and Unwin.

von Grünebaum, G. (1969), *Studien zum Kulturbild und Selbstverständnis des Islams*, Zürich: Artemis.

von Grünebaum, G. (1970), *Classical Islam, 600–1258*, London: George Allen and Unwin.

Hennequin, G. (1977), 'Bonne ou mouvaise monnaie: mutations monétaires et loi de Gresham avant l'époque moderne', *L'Information Historique,* 39, pp. 203–12.
Hennequin, G. (1979), 'Monnaie ou monnayage? en relisant le Traité des monnaies d'Al-Maqrizi' in *Hommages à la mémoire de Serge Sauneron,* Paris, Vol. 1, pp. 317–328.
Islahi, A. (1984), *Economic Thought of Ibn Al-Quayyim,* Jeddah: International Centre for Research in Islamic Economics.
Islahi, A. (1985), 'Ibn Taymiya's Concept of the Market Mechanism', *Journal of Research in Islamic Economics,* 2, (2), pp.55–66, Jeddah.
Lacoste, U. (1969), *Ibn Khaldoun: naissance de l'histoire, passé du Tiers-Monde,* Paris: Maspero.
Lambton, A. (1971), 'Islamic mirrors for Princes' in *La Persia ne Mediovevo,* Rome: Accademia Nazionale dei Lincei.
Langholm, 0. (1979), *Price and Value in the Aristotelian Tradition,* New York: Columbia University Press.
Laoust, H. (1939), 'Essai sur les doctrines sociales et politiques d'Ibn Taymiya', Cairo: IFAO.
Laoust, H. (ed.), (1970), *La Politique de Ghazali,* Paris: Geuthner.
Leaman, 0. (1985), *An Introduction to Medieval Islamic Philosophy,* Cambridge: Cambridge University Press.
Lewis, B. (1937), 'The Islamic Guilds', *Economic History Review,* 8.
Lowry, S. Todd. (1987a), *Pre-classical Economic Thought,* Boston: Kluwer.
Lowry, S. Todd. (1987b), *The Archaeology of Economic Ideas: the Classical Greek Tradition,* Durham, N.C.: Duke University Press.
Mahmasani, S. (1932), *Les idées économiques de Ibn Khaldoun,* Lyon: Bosc Frères.
Mainier, R. (1912), 'Les idées économiques et sociales d'un philosophe arabe du XIVe siècle Ibn Khaldoun', in *Revue d'Histoire Economique et Sociale,* pp.409–26, Paris.
Marçais, G. (1954), 'Considérations sur les villes musulmanes et notamment sur le rôle du muhtasib' in *Receuil de la Société Jean Bodin,* 6, pp.249–61, Paris.
Miller, C. (1925), 'Studien zur Geschichte der Geldlehre', *Münchener Volkswirtschaftliche Studien,* (146), Stuttgart.
Minost, E. (1936), 'Au sujet du traité des monnaies musulmanes de Maqrizi', *Bulletin de l'Institut d'Egypte,* 19, pp. 45–61, Paris
Nassar, N. (1967), *La Pensée réaliste d'Ibn Khaldoun,* Paris: P.U.F.
Oulalou, F. (1976), 'La Pensée socio-economique d'Al-Maqrizi', *Bulletin Economique et Social du Maroc,* 130, pp. 1–136, Rabat.
Peters, F. (1968), *Aristotle and the Arabs,* New York: New York University Press.
Plessner, M. (1928), 'Der Oikonomikos des Neu-pythagoriers Bryson und sein Einfluss auf die Islamische Wissenschaft', Heidelberg: C. Winter.
Qadir, A. (1942), 'The Economic Ideas of Ibn Khaldoun', *The Indian Journal of Political Science,* 22, pp. 898–907, Delhi.
Richter, G. (1932), *Studien zur Geschichte der älteren arabischen Fürstenspiegel,* Leipzig: Leipziger semitistiche Studien.
Ritter, H. (1917), 'Ein arabisches Handbuch der Handelswissenschaft' in *Der Islam,* 7.
Rosenthal, E. (1965), *Averroës' Commentary on Plato's Republic,* Cambridge: Cambridge University Press.
Salman, D. (1939), 'The Medieval Latin Translations of Alfarabi's Works', in *The New Scholasticism,* vol. 13, pp. 245–61.
Schumpeter, J. (1954), *History of Economic Analysis,* New York: Oxford University Press.
Sharif, M. (1955), 'Ibn Khaldoun the Pioneer Economist', *Islamic Literature,* 6, (5), pp. 33–40.
Sherwani, H. (1956), 'Ibn Taymiya's Economic Thought', *The Islamic Literature,* 8, (1), pp. 9–23, Lahore.
Sherwani, H. (1970), 'Ibn Khaldoun and his Political Economic Thought', *Islamic Culture,* 44, (2), pp. 71–80.
Siddiqi, M. (1981), *Muslim Economic Thinking: A Survey of Contemporary Literature,* Jeddah: International Centre for Research in Islamic Economics.
Siddiqi, M. (1982), *Recent Works on the History of Economic Thought in Islam: A Survey,* Jeddah: International Centre for Research in Islamic Economics.

Sourdel, D. (1959), *Le Vizirat Abbaside de 749–936*, 2 vol., Damascus: Institut Français de Damas.
Spengler, J. (1963), 'Economic Thought of Islam: Ibn Khaldoun' in *Comparative Studies in Society and History*, (6), pp. 268–305.
Syed, A. (1970), 'Economics of Ibn Khaldoun: a Selection', *Africa Quarterly*, **10**, (3), pp. 251–9, Delhi.

2 Information and risk in the medieval doctrine of usury during the thirteenth century

André Lapidus[1]

Introduction

The medieval doctrine of usury[2] seems to present contradictory pictures.[3] A modern reader could, without probing into the texts too deeply, find both a positive explanation of interest and a rejection of such an explanation, as well as positions both justifying and prohibiting interest on loans. These contradictory pictures have surely enabled modern economists to find apparent antecedents, discovering, for instance, the genesis of the idea that only business profit raises interest above zero (Schumpeter, 1954, p. 105) or that underemployment could be efficiently fought by increasing the incentive to invest, which implies lowering interest rates. (The latter argument, found in Sommerville (1931), was taken up by Keynes (1973, pp. 351–2).) Of course, such readings of the works of schoolmen surely helped to make some historians of medieval thought go bald.

My purpose in this paper is to stem their hair loss. While using the categories of economic analysis, it is not my intention to discover a first draft of modern economic theory in these thirteenth century writings. Instead I propose to add to our understanding of how and why medieval representations of negotiation, information, property and risk differ from ours and to reconstruct their internal consistency.

The result of the operation is a play with three characters: a creditor, a debtor and a moralist (who could be a theologian or a canonist). The moralist has knowledge which is more or less shared by the other two characters. This means that he has one or several competing theories of interest which exclude other theories. Whether or not, as a moralist, he has to accept or reject some kind of interest is a different question. But, in so far as he is an actor in the play, he has to tell the other two characters what they ought to do and he cannot therefore avoid dealing with this question.

The first act of the play unfolds in a riskless context. It shows that a negotiation problem between creditor and debtor generates an indeterminacy that could be solved through a just price approach. But – for the show must go on – the existence of such a price, which conforms with the moralist's knowledge, guarantees neither that this price would be accepted, nor that it could easily be calculated. A problem of estimation and of control then arises, the solution to which is first conceived in terms of a rigorous prohibition of usury. But for the clever creditor the existence of a range of substitutes to usurious operations allows him to shift to perfectly licit transactions. Hence, the moralist's control has to be tightened. This is achieved by using property in order to discriminate licit from usurious transactions. End of Act I.

Surely, if the creditor here plays the part of the villain, he is not short of resources, and he is able to imagine numerous ways of asserting ownership when there is none. Risk associated with property, justifying the claim for a special income, then corresponds to the moralist's line of response in the second Act. But a problem presents itself. Usually the creditor knows how risky his operation is. Why then should he share his information with the debtor, or, even if he does, why should he reveal it to the moralist? The latter's numerous attempts to give a proper answer – agreement between both parties, recourse to an expert – are far from being fully satisfactory. Some contracts happen to be especially appealing – for example, the kinds of contract in which the risk depends on the behaviour of one of the parties and governs the income or quantities to be exchanged. In such cases, the moralist can anticipate retirement when he will be able to concentrate on much more important matters such as, for instance, the number of angels that could stand on the head of a pin. But the story of the pin is another play in which information and risk do not belong to the scenery.

Usury in a riskless context

Usury as a sin of intention: a problem of indeterminacy
If questions of information and risk are so involved in medieval doctrine, it is because usury, far from being merely a material fact, is firstly a sin of intention. The mere perception of an income received by a lender beyond his capital is never sufficient to support a conclusion that the loan is usurious. In the early thirteenth century, William of Auxerre, for example, defined usury as 'the intention to receive something more in a loan than the capital' (William of Auxerre, *Summa Aurea*, t. 48, c.l, q.l). A similar idea can be found in Robert of Courçon: 'usury is a sin resulting from the fact of receiving or *aiming at* receiving something above the principal' (Robert of Courçon, *De Usura*, p. 3, my italics; see also pp. 13, 57, 61 and 78). It must be stressed that these lines were written before the full diffusion in the Christian Western World of the Latin translation of Aristotle's works in political and moral philosophy by Robert Grosseteste or William of Moerbeke. Church doctrine on usury had longstanding roots, which were independent of those related to the Aristotelian thesis about the sterility of money, or to the so-called 'classical argument' developed by Thomas Aquinas.[4] In spite of a growing consensus about the

importance of pre-Thomistic arguments – such as the Roman law framework of money loans – the normative dimension of the doctrine of usury has often been underestimated on the grounds that its analytic content is allegedly poor.

However, a careful examination shows that the analytic content is not so poor. The main roots are to be found in patristic literature. The Greek and Latin Church Fathers told, in various ways, the same instructive story: that of a consumption loan given by a rich man who is widely provided for in all necessities, to a poor man for whom the loan is a condition of survival. Later, most scholastic thinkers[5] considered such a loan to be usurious, even though it rested on 'voluntary agreement' of both parties. In their view, the agreement, though voluntary, was 'absolute' for the lender, but 'conditioned' for the borrower. Usury was unambiguously condemned in this case[6] but for reasons that were rather complex.

In its simplest aspect, the money loan was analysed as an intertemporal exchange between the supplier of a present good – the lender, and the supplier of a future good – the borrower. When recognizing the voluntary dimension of the operation for both parties, scholastic thinkers conceded that the exchange could be mutually advantageous.[7] So, the difficulty arose from the way the gain of exchange was to be shared between the creditor and the debtor. As long as we limit ourselves to a single bilateral transaction, every contemporary economist knows that the present – or future – ratio of exchange between a present good and a future good remains undetermined. The solution can be reached through cooperation and depends on the negotiating power of both agents.

Herein lies the first asymmetry: the supplier of the present good – the rich man – was supposed to be vested with a greater power of negotiation than the supplier of the future good – the poor man. It was, then, easy to understand that the lender would be able to appropriate most of the surplus emerging from the exchange. As early as the fourth century, Gregory of Nazianze denounced 'the one who contaminated the soil with usury and interest, amassing where he did not sow and harvesting where he did not scatter seeds, taking his affluence not from the cultivation of the earth but from the destitution of the poor' (*Patrologie Grecque*, t. 35, col. 957, cited by Bernard, 1950, col. 2324). As a practical matter, however, this formulation was problematic. The fourteenth century, for instance, provided several examples of loans in which the borrower was the Prince, with the greater power of negotiation on his side, because the lenders might be threatened with the loss of their capital if not of their lives.

But as a consequence of this instructive story, usury – though morally condemned – was recognized as a surplus from exchange to which both parties might have some claims but which was likely captured by the creditor. Hence, two questions arose, but were so often mixed together in the writings of medieval theologians and jurists that modern commentators have, understandably, been confused by them. The first question was a positive one: what is the non-usurious ratio of exchange between present and future goods? The second question was normative: how can rules of the game be set to get as close as possible to a non-usurious ratio of exchange? Answering these two questions separately will lead us to a resolution of the obvious contradiction between the rigorous prohibition of usury invoked each time a creditor received any income above his capital, and the numerous justifications of interest often presented by the same authors.

Just price and estimation: from one indeterminacy to another

That the ratio of exchange between a present and a future good is significantly greater than one was at least implicitly recognized by the major scholastic thinkers of the thirteenth century – herein lay a justification for the presence of extrinsic titles alongside the main loan contract, the *mutuum* – and this recognition was explicit for some of them. Such was the position of Thomas Aquinas: 'One harms one's neighbour when preventing him from collecting what he legitimately hoped to possess. And then, the compensation has not to be founded on equality because a future possession is not worth a present possession' (Thomas Aquinas, *Summa Theologica*, II–II, q. 62, a. 4, resp. 2). His disciple, Giles of Lessines, explained in a Böhm-Bawerkian fashion that 'Future goods are not evaluated at the same (present) price as the same goods immediately available, even if they could later be of great utility' (Giles of Lessines, *De Usuris*, c. 9).

Such a position revealed an interesting shift from an analysis that treated a loan as a negotiation problem, the solution to which was *ex ante* undetermined. When saying that a future good has a lower present value than a present good, one might solve the problem through a just price approach. Attention could thus be focused on the social evaluation of goods, and not on the relative bargaining strength of the respective parties in an isolated transaction (see Lapidus, 1987, chap. I). But the most prominent justification for the difference between the values of present and future goods was linked to risk (which will be discussed later). First, however, let us concentrate on the explanation of intertemporal exchange in the absence of uncertainty.[8]

The usual explanation underlined the loss suffered in such an exchange by the supplier of the present good. Through the doctrine of *damnum emergens* (or loss incurred), this sacrifice was characterized as an opportunity cost in terms of the consumption forgone by the lender which might legitimately be compensated by interest. The perspective was widened with the introduction of the doctrine of *lucrum cessans* (or profit ceasing). This referred to the opportunity cost incurred by a lender – in the form of forgone profits – when resources transferred to the borrower would otherwise have been used for the lender's own business. These two extrinsic titles, as Noonan (1957, p. 116) has pointed out, were not really discussed before the middle of the thirteenth century (with the exception of Robert of Courçon who condemned *lucrum cessans*; *De Usura*, pp. 61–3). They need, as a prerequisite, general agreement about the use of the *mutuum* as the formal frame for a money loan, and an appreciation of the Thomistic understanding of money. Thomas Aquinas, in spite of a certain mistrust – chiefly aimed at the *lucrum cessans* – clearly stated the principles on which they were grounded: 'In his contract with the borrower, the lender may, without any sin, stipulate an indemnity to be paid for the prejudice he suffers while being deprived of what was his possession; this is not to sell the use of money, but to receive a compensation. Besides, the loan may spare the borrower a greater loss than the one to which the lender is exposed. It is thus with his benefit that the first makes up the loss of the second' (Thomas Aquinas, *Summa Theologica*, II–II, q. 78, a. 2, ad. 1).

But, if the principle of a difference between present and future goods – which would potentially justify transactions involving interest payments – was quite clear-cut, the estimation of this difference remained difficult to determine.[9] As this issue was approached as a just price problem, subjective evaluations of opportunity costs could not be appropriate. It seemed difficult to find a way between the simple recognition of a 'common estimation'[10] and the rough intuition of an internal rate of return for productive goods,[11] the importance of which increased as soon as scholastic writers began to consider some kinds of intertemporal exchange as an exchange between a present good and a present right to receive future goods.[12]

The difficulty in establishing the proper value of future goods – even if acknowledged to be inferior to the value of present goods – was not based on a lack of information about the things to be exchanged themselves. It stemmed instead from the limited ability of men to devise a precise calculation of the differential magnitudes. *Ex ante* indeterminacy of the ratio of exchange was thus not eliminated by intertemporal opportunity cost considerations, even in a riskless context.

Normative analysis: the consistency of the rigorous prohibition of usury in question

This leads us to a normative analysis that will shed light on the apparently contradictory positions among scholastic thinkers or, for that matter, to what seem to be contradictions within the writings of some of them. Although Thomas Aquinas, for instance, set out the reasons why a future good had to be estimated at less than a present good, he strongly forbade the seller from increasing his price in a credit sale: 'To sell a thing above its just price because one allows the buyer a delay of payment is an obvious usury because the allowed delay has the characteristics of a loan. Consequently, all that is required above the just price for this delay is like the price or the interest of a loan, and thus must be considered as usurious' (Thomas Aquinas, *Summa Theologica*, II–II, q. 78, a. 2, sol. 7).

Another example of apparent contradiction can be found in the interpretation of the *census*. This practice, developed in the thirteenth century, involved a transaction in which one party advanced cash to a second party on the understanding that the latter would be obliged to make annual payments thereafter. The seller of the *census* was thus in a position of a borrower with commitments to service the debt over time, while the buyer of the *census* was in the position of a lender. Initially, the annual payments were expected to be made in kind from the fruitful use of the property – such as land or cattle – against which the buyer had advanced the funds.[13] Later the annual instalments were made in cash. But what was the nature of such transactions? More than one interpretation was possible. Some regarded the *census* as a sale of property – not a loan – and therefore licit, the position taken by Giles of Lessines (*De Usuris*, c. 9) and Alexander Lombard (*Tractatus de Usuris*, c. 7, par. 79). Others treated the pecuniary census as a loan and thus usurious; for example, Henry of Ghent (*Quodlibet* II, q. 15, cited by Hamelin, 1962, p. 94, n. 80) and Robert of Courçon (*De Usura*, p. 63).

The issue faced by the moralist was a typical 'agency problem' in which he played the part of the principal while the creditor was the agent. Conceivably, a full analysis of the transaction might involve prohibitive costs of calculation for both the principal and the agent. In that event, the principal might be inclined to simplify matters by imposing a stern rule forbidding any transaction in which there was a difference between the capital lent and paid back. This decision could be costless for the principal and highly efficient (for the agent could be charged with a mortal sin). And it might be based on *a priori* judgement that any repayment by a borrower in excess of the funds advanced would be suspect as usurious as a consequence of the superior bargaining strength of a creditor. Of course, this does not contradict the understanding of interest as a morally and analytically admissible economic category.

But this position would not be easy to sustain. A major difficulty stemmed from the existence of a large set of transactions that were close substitutes for an interest loan (for example, credit sales, *societas* (or business partnership), bank deposits, and so on) when they were not, like the *census* discussed above, alternatively interpretable as interest loans. And some of these transactions seemed to exhibit a calculable legitimate surplus. As the imagination of merchants and financiers in the Middle Ages seemed unlimited, the field covered by a strict prohibition of interest loans ran the risk of becoming smaller and smaller. Some technique for partitioning the larger set of transactions into those that were legitimate and those that were usurious was needed. Property was soon to become a crucial ingredient in the development of this line of analysis.

Property against usury

After the rediscovery of Roman law in Italian universities, a free contract for fungible goods – the *mutuum* – fixed the legal framework for money loans. This was later to become the centrepiece for the Thomistic analysis of usury. Formally the contract itself precluded any interest being paid on a money loan. Robert of Courçon, at the very beginning of the thirteenth century, explained the mechanism by writing that 'the name of the *mutuum* comes, indeed, from that which was mine [*meum*] becomes yours [*tuum*] or inversely. As soon as the five shillings that you lent me become mine, property passes from you to me. It would then be an injustice if, for a good which is mine, you were to receive something; for you are not entitled to any return from that which is my possession' (Robert of Courçon, *De Usura*, p. 15). Sixty years later, Thomas Aquinas completed the argument, showing that contractual interest on a money loan, mentioned in the loan contract itself, was impossible because this contract could be nothing but the *mutuum* (Lapidus, 1987, pp. 1097–1103).

The interesting idea here was that only private property rights justified a return on a good. Because the *mutuum* was conceived as a transfer of ownership of money, the new owner – the borrower – could not be obliged to pay an interest on what was now his. (The borrower might still, however, be obliged to pay compensation for the opportunity cost imposed on the lender as a result of the transfer of ownership – as in *damnum emergens* and *lucrum cessans*.) But the idea of private property was still not unambiguously articulated. Since the fifth century, of course, Christianity had given up the communism of Church Fathers such as Ambrosio or John Chrysostome. Even so, for most schoolmen (except notably Alexander of Hales or John Duns Scotus), private property had not achieved the status of a natural right, or what we would call today full property rights, exclusive and transferable. From Augustine, we know already that property rights came from human law and it was in this way that Gratian introduced it into Canon Law in about 1140. Still more, for Thomas Aquinas private property was nothing but an institution stemming from *jus gentium*, that is, a supplement that human reason brought to natural law, mainly for considerations of efficiency. Further, it should be noted that feudal society was characterized by a complex network of property links which directed the owners of many goods to manage them as prescribed by the *jus procurandi et dispensadi* (that is, not exclusively in accordance with their private interests, but also in accordance with the wider interests of the community).

The latter considerations helped to provide guidance in judging whether or not a transaction formally equivalent to an interest loan was usurious. A surplus might be collected by the owner but, to be non-usurious, the transaction and the amount of the surplus must not contradict the socially recognized goals of the community. Many remarks of schoolmen confirm this point. Within this perspective, at the beginning of the fourteenth century, Alexander Lombard acknowledged the legitimacy of exchange operations which previously had been firmly prohibited.[14] And, in some cases, the activity of a merchant or of a financier was analysed as a private alternative to a direct intervention of the State, which would be useful for the community: 'The merchant may earn as much as the just and good legislator should attribute to any public servant: if the legislator does not come to his aid, the merchant may make this profit without it being an extortion. For if there were a good legislator in a country in need, he should rent such kinds of merchants for a high price in order that they provide and store necessary goods: and not only should he supply them and their families with necessities but he should, moreover, remunerate their labour, their experience and all the risks they are running' (John Duns Scotus, *In Quattuor Libros Sententiarum*, dist. 15, q. 2, 21).

Ambiguities about individual entitlements to property, however, remained. Some contracts, by their very nature (like the *mutuum*) transferred property in a way that clearly identified the owner. Others left open the possibility of manipulation about the actual ownership or presupposed common property shared by both parties to the transaction. In the latter case, the identification of each individual's property was not obvious, nor was each one's right and contribution to the product of the operation. The *societas* (or partnership) illustrates this. In Roman law, the *societas* was an association between persons who engaged their labour, money or goods in a profitable operation. The income of each member of the *societas* depended, naturally, on its result. Every type of sharing was allowed till the Middle Ages, when the case of one partner bearing the entire responsibility in case of loss was proscribed.[15]

The moralist who was asked to reach a decision about the licitness of a *societas* thus had to discover the actual sharing of the property which might be hidden behind the formal terms of the contract. And, of course, he did not have at his disposal the information known by the partner who was interested in dissimulating it. In other words, he was faced with a problem analogous to what might be called today a 'moral hazard'.

Usury, risk and information

Property and risk: the claim for non usurious income
The 'moral hazard' problem arising from asymmetric information might be addressed if a method could be found to induce the agents to reveal the true nature of their property interests. The penalty for failure to do so would be the loss of right to an income. For most schoolmen, despite several nuances, the incidence of risk-bearing came to be the criterion of the legitimacy of claims to income. They presupposed that many operations were already taking place in a risky context and held that the total or partial rejection of risk-bearing should mean the total or partial rejection of a future possibility of gain.

It must be borne in mind that the conception of risk presented here substantially differs from the lack of knowledge which, as was discussed above, results from insufficient ability to calculate future values. Risk concerns states of the world conditioned by future events, the occurrence of which is not certain. The same Alexander Lombard would later write that 'all things being equal, a riskful thing is worth less than a riskless thing' (Alexander Lombard, c. 7, par. 67). Although risk-bearing revealed property, it did not follow that all property was, by nature, subject to risk. The case of riskless rent, studied by Aegidius Romanus (see Noonan, 1957, p. 59) is the simplest illustration of this point.

But the association of property and risk raised another question. In medieval terms, one could ask whether the distinction between them was a 'real distinction' or only a 'distinction of reason'. In the first case, there was no basis for preventing property and risk being sold separately as two different sources of income. In the second case, on the other hand, no separation was permissible, nor was it even certain that risk-bearing could claim any specific income. A certain evolution in the representations of the connection between risk and property can be identified, although no significant change occurred before the end of the thirteenth century. Indeed, the period seems to have been dominated by a kind of standard understanding, confirmed by Thomistic analysis, stating that, whereas property and use could be separated – and sold separately – for non-consumptible goods only, risk always remained inseparable from property, although its claim to an income was sometimes justified and considered separately. However, this representation led progressively to a segregated treatment of use, property and risk.

In the development of this perspective, a significant event, not directly connected with risk and hardly connected with usury, was a decretal, originating from Pope Nicholas III around 1280, which stated that members of the Franciscan Order who used material goods did not transgress their rule of poverty because the use of these goods had to be separated from their ownership (*Decretals*, Liber Sextus, 1.5, tit. 11, c. 3, *Exiit qui seminat*). Hence, the real link between property and use, even for consumptible goods, was broken. This led to the idea that among the characteristics of a good, some, which could be conceptualized separately, could also be sold and bought separately. Risk was clearly one of them. This helped to account for the wide acceptance of risk as an autonomous source of income from the end of the thirteenth century onwards. In this respect, it is interesting to note the parallel evolution of the discussion of the *census*, which was gradually seen less as analogous to either a credit sale or as a shared property, and more as an exchange between a present good and a right to future payments. Accordingly, Alexander Lombard justified life *census* on the basis of the pure risk – the uncertainty about the duration of life – accepted by the seller (Alexander Lombard, *Tractatus de Usuris*, c. 7, par. 81).

To a certain extent, the outcome of this evolution emerged much later, in the fifteenth century, with the generalization of the sale of risk through insurance contracts, previously ignored by Roman law (see Bensa, 1897). This clearly ratified the divorce between property, use and risk.

The incidence of risk in the nature of a transaction
The most convenient starting point for the analysis of the incidence of risk in a transaction is the well-known decretal *Naviganti* by Pope Gregory IX:

> Somebody lending a certain quantity of money to one sailing or going to a fair in order to receive something beyond the capital, for he takes the risk upon himself, is to be thought a usurer. Also the one who gives ten shillings to receive after a certain time the same measure of grain, wine or oil, though it is then worth more, when one really doubts whether it will be worth more or less at the date of delivery, must not, for that, be considered a usurer. Because of this doubt again, the one who sells bread, grain, wine, oil or other commodities so that he receives after a certain period of time more than they are worth then, is excused if, in lack of a forward contract, they would not have been sold (*Decretals*, 1.5, tit. 19, c. 19, *Naviganti*).

This decretal is highly questionable (see McLaughlin (1939, pp. 103–4) or Noonan (1957, pp. 137 ff)). At first glance, it seems to adopt successively two opposing positions concerning risk. The first sentence condemns the sea loan (*foenus nauticum*), while the concluding sentences allow a discount if the future value of the commodity to be sold is uncertain, and an increase in the case of a credit sale. The difference in treatment is large enough to have led some commentators to suggest that the condemnation of the *foenus nauticum* could have arisen from an error in transcription by the Pope's secretary, Raymond of Peñaforte. But a closer examination suggests a consistent position. The key to the first statement is the expression 'is to be thought a usurer' (*usurarius est censendus*). One must keep in mind that usury is a sin of intention. Thus, in the *foenus nauticum*, the receipt of any income by the lender is not in itself usurious. The problem in such a situation is that an external observer, such as the theologian, is far from being certain that the lender does not overestimate the risk of the operation to disguise a usurious benefit as a legitimate income.

Besides this 'moral hazard' interpretation,[16] it should also be noted that the *foenus nauticum* is not a simple operation, in which only two states of the world can occur – the freight arrives safe and sound or perishes at sea. Even if the freight is intact, the merchant will run another risk when selling it. And this latter risk is not taken into account in the contract between the creditor and his debtor. Thus, in the event that the ship does not sink, one party has to assume the entire responsibility if a loss occurs at the point of sale. Selling overseas depended on the capital advanced – which belonged to the creditor for the duration of the crossing – and there is no reason for this ownership to be transferred to the debtor during the second phase of the operation. In spite of its name, the sea loan (*foenus nauticum*) is clearly not a loan[17] but rather similar to a kind of partnership which allowed common ownership of money invested in a presumably profitable operation. This strictly prohibited any partner from escaping, at any moment, from responsibility for a possible loss.[18]

Once again, the main point seems to have been the link between property and risk. Apart from his own interpretation of *Naviganti*, this was well stated by Raymond of Peñaforte, in a commentary in which he tried to synthesize the differences between usurious and licit transactions. Raymond pointed out three distinctions dealing with

1. the link between ownership and risk
2. the consumption of the good through use
3. the sterility of the good[19].

The latter two characteristics constituted the grounds on which the scholastic theory of interest and money was built.[20] But the first played a different role. It served a discriminatory function. Raymond of Peñaforte suggested that among apparently licit transactions, some could be usurious for the owner did not take the risk upon himself.

This rule of association between risk and property hence provided an incentive to the actual owner to reveal his (riskful) property – otherwise he could not ask for an income from it – and forbade a formal owner from receiving income from an operation in which he bore no risk.

The effectiveness of risk and the efficiency of the rule
The efficiency of the rule associating property and risk closely depends on identifying the extent of the risk involved. Here again, the information may not be symmetric between the creditor and the debtor, either of whom may have at his disposal far better information than the other. Similarly, the moralist, who had to decide about the licitness of the transaction may be imperfectly informed.

This idea is well expressed in the doctrine of *venditio sub dubio* – referring to real doubt at the time of sale about the future value of goods – as applied to credit sales or to advance payment for merchandise to be delivered later. The terms on which these operations were permitted were explained in two rulings, the already cited decretal *Naviganti* and the decretal *In civitate*.[21]

In civitate is the older of the two. It reintroduced the terms of a letter written in 1175 by Pope Alexander III to the Archbishop of Genoa, in which the case of people who buy pepper or cinnamon today but promise to pay later at a higher price is discussed. 'Although arrangements of that kind and of that form', wrote

Alexander III, 'could not strictly be called usury, sellers are nevertheless exposed to being considered as guilty, unless they could really doubt the plus or minus value of the commodities at the time of payment' (*Decretals*, 1.5, tit. 19, c.6, *In civitate*). Similarly, in *Naviganti*, Gregory IX argued that a 'real doubt' about the future value of a good allowed its price to be decreased when payment in advance of delivery was made. It must be stressed that the cases discussed here are quite distinct from those of the present price of a future good when no uncertainty occurred; they are also distinct from a perfectly anticipated difference between future and present values of the same good. The question debated here concerned uncertainty about future values. Therefore, if time influenced the value of things it is not as pure time, which was definitely excluded (see Thomas Aquinas, *Summa Theologica*, II–II, q. 78, a. 2, sol. 7), but as risk over time.

The analysis of transactions subject to *venditio sub dubio* clearly involved an assessment of the magnitude of risk before the absence of usurious intention could be established. But there was a possibility of divergence between the risk perceived by the seller on the basis of private information and the riskiness as perceived by the buyer and the moralist. Nearly all the commentators on the two decretals saw the difficulty. Consequently, the moralist had to find a way to discover the hidden information or to force its owner to behave as he would have if it were common information. Already in *Naviganti*, Gregory IX introduced a supplementary condition in case of payment in advance – that the seller actually intended to sell his good later – but this was of no help in revealing what was in the mind of the seller. Nor did the condition imposed by Giles of Lessines that 'the same doubt exists for both parties, on the question of knowing whether one receives, or will receive, more or less', achieve this purpose (Giles of Lessines, *De Usuris*, c. 9). Nothing will compel any party, except respect for a religious requirement or fear of a punishment, to reveal private information. A possible solution, efficient but difficult to manage, would be resort to an expert – a typical medieval solution – each time a question of evaluation arose. In this respect, William of Auxerre wrote that when 'the seller sells on credit his commodities for a higher price than that which they were worth at the time of the contract, and sells them according to the estimation of wise men knowing this type of contracts, the contract is not usurious' (William of Auxerre, *Summa Aurea*, De Usura, c. 3, q. 2).

On the other hand, the outcomes of other contracts could be affected by the behaviour of one of the parties.[22] Beyond the uncertainties about the delivery of goods, about prices of goods in the future, and about the course of external events – cases previously examined – risk could arise from the actions of agents. The debtor, for example, might fail to repay the loan when due. Similarly, a partner in a *societas* might not exert himself as expected. The existence of such a moral hazard was clearly perceived by several schoolmen and this explained, for instance, Thomas Aquinas's suspicion of insurance, for it invited the insured party to be lax in taking care of his property (*Summa Theologica*, II–II, q. 66, a.2, resp.).

As is well known, a solution to this sort of problem can be approached by attempting to establish a scheme of incentives within which the potential beneficiary of a moral hazard would have an incentive to protect his partner's interest. Most of the contracts that were recognized as licit achieved that status precisely because they included such incentives. The licitness of a *societas*, as has already been pointed out, rested on more stringent conditions than in Roman law, namely, the impossibility of one or some partners avoiding any risk of loss while others bore it in its entirety. Hence all parties had a stake in the success of the enterprise.

Similarly, *poena conventionalis* – a penalty by common agreement – was validated. This contractual practice, as an extrinsic title to the *mutuum*, stipulated that a daily indemnity should be paid by a debtor to dissuade him from exceeding the time limit of a loan. Designed to protect the creditor, its counterpart was that it might also threaten the debtor, and in two different ways. First, the duration of the loan might be so short that the borrower could not possibly pay back on time. Naturally, this practice was condemned, but the fault was not so easy to establish. Second, the creditor might raise the indemnity specified in the contract to a level exceeding the opportunity cost of the non-availability of his money at the expiry date. Some scholastic authors attacked this point in a rigorous way. This was true of Raymond of Peñaforte, who declared that 'if the penalty proceeds from a convention, that is from a common agreement between the parties mentioned in the contract, so that at least the fear of this penalty forced payment at the expiry date, there is no usury'.[23] John Duns Scotus, some sixty years later, was still more precise when writing: 'an obvious sign that a penalty is not usurious is the following: the merchant prefers to have his money back at the expiry date rather than the day after, accompanied by a penalty' (John Duns Scotus, *In IV Libros Sententiarum*, Opus oxoniensis, IV, dist. 15, q. 2, 18).

The discussions about the *societas* and *poena* marked an important analytical step. They showed that the schoolmen had become conscious that a proper scheme of incentives – embodied in the terms of a contract – could provide a filter for non-usurious operations. Such an approach, in turn, could spare them from close personal scrutiny of each individual transaction. Their victory was not complete, but the battles could be expected to become less ferocious.

The authors of the thirteenth century already knew from Augustine what was later to be forgotten, by Bernard de Mandeville, for instance: that trade is not, by nature, dishonest. But the discussions about usury showed that the suspicion of a fraudulent intention progressively escaped from the initial discussion about money lending to contaminate nearly every economic activity, as long as imperfect information opened the door to strategic behaviour. The schoolmen's answer sounds then like a Promethean project, for only God, wrote Hostiensis, 'questions the heart and not the hand'.[24] The purpose of the various devices involved in the prohibition of usury was, indeed, to force the hand to reveal the content of the heart – for want of a direct investigation. As a question in economic theory, the prohibition of usury did not survive the domination of the Church's teaching on the understanding of economic activities. Only the Promethean project remained.

Notes

1. A first draft of this paper was read at the *Seminaire de la Salle de Statistiques* in Paris (April 1989). I would like to thank the participants in this seminar for helpful comments and, especially, Annie L. Cot, Daniel Diatkine, Stephanie Flood, Jerome Lallement, S. Todd Lowry and Antoin Murphy.
2. Among the secondary references to the doctrine of usury employed in this chapter, I have drawn upon Bernard (1950), De Roover (1971, chap. 6), Dumas (1953), Langholm (1984), Lapidus (1987), Mélitz (1971), Nelson (1949, chaps. 1 and 2), Noonan (1957), Spicq (1935, pp. 440–86), Viner (1978, pp . 85–99). Though the importance of information and risk, as related to usury, has been widely recognized (see Noonan (1957, chap. 6) on risk-sharing investment), it has never, with the exception of Chiquet, Huyghes Despointes and Schneider (1987), given rise to a systematic account.
3. The period dealt with in this paper goes from the mid-twelfth century with the *Decretum* by Gratian and ends in the first years of the fourteenth century with the *Tractatus De Usuris* by Alexander Lombard.
4. Chiefly in *Summa Theologica*, II–II, q . 78, but also in *De Malo*, q. 13, a. 4. The question of the consistency of the classical argument is discussed in Melitz (1971) and Lapidus (1987).
5. See the example given by Robert of Courçon in which a poor man is not guilty of usury when he is obliged to contract a loan and pay interest (*De Usura*, pp. 17–19).
6. The various decisions of the popes and of the councils were introduced in the *Corpus Juris Canonici* by Gratian first, in about 1140 (*Decret*, I, dist. 46, c. 9, 10; dist. 47, c. 1–8; II, causa 14, q. 1, c. 2; q. 3, c. 1–4; q. 4, c. 1–12) and later by Popes Gregory IX (*Decretals*, 1.5, tit. 19), Boniface VIII (*ibid.*, Liber Sextus, 1.5, tit. 5) and Clement V (*ibid.*, Constitutiones, 1.5, tit. 5). It is with this last Pope that the condemnation of usury reached its climax, for Clement V promulgated a decretal at the Council of Vienna in 1311 where he decided to punish as heretics those who declared that usury was not a sin.
7. The idea that trade is mutually advantageous is not specific to the analysis of usury. It clearly comes from the theory of the just price. Thomas Aquinas, for instance, wrote that 'purchasing and selling were instituted for the common good of both parties, for each one needs the other's products and reciprocally' (*In Decem Libros Ethicorum*, l.V, lect. 9, c; see also *Summa Theologica*, II–II, q. 77, a. 1, resp. and, in Aristotle, *Nicomachean Ethica*, Bk V, v).
8. This distinction may at times be observed in the structure of the works of certain writers. In the chapter of the *Summa Aurea* on usurious contracts (1.3, t. 48, c. 3) William of Auxerre, for instance, treated in question 1 the case of term certainty and in question 2 the case of term uncertainty.
9. Alternatively, the estimation of this difference is easy to obtain only in very specific cases. See, for instance, the description of a non-usurious forward sale by Giles of Lessines: 'Time can be linked with certain transactions of goods for it can add something to or, on the contrary, take something away from the proper value of these goods. In this sense, if somebody, owing to time, sells more or less than at the just price, such a contract is not

usurious. For a measure of corn is justly assessed as being worth more in summer than in autumn, all things being equal' (*De Usuris*, c. 9).

10. Generally revealed by the 'estimation of a good upright man', as in William of Auxerre's *Summa Aurea* (1.3, t. 48, c. 3, q. 2).

11. A current idea about the *census* – an arrangement under which cash was advanced in exchange for annual payments thereafter – was that it had to be capitalized eight times its annual return (see Noonan, 1957, p. 156). Still on this most controversial question, Alexander Lombard wrote that 'when you evaluate the just price, it is sufficient to look at the price for the buyer and for his descendants up to a certain level, for example his sons or grandsons. But one must not consider all his descendants, until the end of time, otherwise the good on sale could not be estimated' (*Tractatus de Usuris*, c. 7, par. 87).

12. This was how the *census* was understood. See Giles of Lessines (De Usuris, c. 9) or Alexander Lombard (*Tractatus de Usuris*, c. 7, par. 101).

13. On the development of the analysis of the *census*, see Noonan (1957, pp. 154–70) or, up to Alexander Lombard, Hamelin (1962, pp. 91–7).

14. Alexander Lombard, *Tractatus de Usuris*, c. 7, par. 139.

15. Robert of Courçon expressed this by writing that 'every merchant contracting with another for trading must, if he wishes to participate in the profits, show that he participates in the danger and expenses which attend all buying and selling' (*De Usura*, p. 73).

16. Such a reading of *Naviganti* is suggested by Goffredus of Trani (see McLaughlin (1939, p. 103) or Noonan (1957, p. 139)).

17. In this respect, it must be remembered that in Roman law, the *foenus nauticum* could be paid with the benefits of the operation (*Digest*, 22, 21, 5). This explains the apparent confusion between *foenus nauticum* and *societas* by such canonists as Hostiensis. For an opposite point of view, see Noonan (1957, pp. 138–43).

18. The general principle was stated by Thomas Aquinas in the following way: 'The one committing his money to a merchant or a craftsman by means of some kind of partnership does not transfer the property of his money to him, but it remains his possession; so that at his (the creditor's) risk, the merchant trades or the craftsman works with it; and he can thus licitly seek a part of the profit as coming from his own property' (*Summa Theologica*, II–II, q. 78, a. 2, obj. 5).

19. 'Gregory sets three differences between loan and rent; first, in a loan, risk is transferred to the one who receives, which is not the case in a rent; second, money is not destroyed by use as a house or a horse or another rented thing; third, the use of money brings neither fruit nor utility to the user, contrary to a field, a house or another rented thing' (Raymond of Peñaforte, *Summa de Casibus Conscientiae*, 1.2, par. 7, 7).

20. Nonetheless, the treatment of consumptibility is typically pre-Thomistic, for it argues that money cannot give birth to profit because it is not destroyed through use. The argument of Thomas Aquinas – as well as some earlier treatments, by Robert of Courçon, for instance – is exactly the opposite as it rests on the idea that it is because money is destroyed through use – buying commodities – that the creditor cannot remain its owner (see Thomas Aquinas, *Summa Theologica*, II–II, q.78, a.1, resp.; Robert of Courçon, *De Usura*, p.15).

21. Robert of Courçon, as he frequently did, anticipated a position about future contracts which was to be later commonly accepted. See *De Usura*, pp. 57–61.

22. In the same way, Chiquet, Huyghes Despointes and Schneider (1987, chap. 2) distinguished two kinds of contracts: those with extrinsic and those with intrinsic risk.

23. *Summa de Casibus Conscientiae*, II, par. 5. See also Robert of Courçon (*De Usura*, pp. 65–7) who admitted interest in the *poena* under the condition that it was given to the poor.

24. *Commentaria super Quinque Libros Decretalium*, V, 19, 6; cited by Noonan (1957, p. 92).

References

Alexander Lombard (Alexander of Alexandria), 'Tractatus de Usuris', in Hamelin, A-M. (ed.) (1962), *Un Traité de Morale Économique au XIVème Siècle*, Louvain/Montreal/Lille: Nauwelaerts/Librairie Franciscaine/Giard.

Bensa, E. (1897), *'Histoire de contrat d'assurance au Moyen-Age*, Paris: A. Fontemoing.
Bernard, A. (1950), 'La Formation de la doctrine ecclésiastique sur l'usure', in Vacant, A.,
   Mangenot, E., Amann, E., (eds), *Dictionnaire de théologie Catholique*, vol. .XV(2), Paris:
   Letouzey et Ané.
Chiquet, C., Huyghes Despointes, H. and Schneider, J.-L. (1987), 'La Perception du risque au
   treizième siècle', unpublished dissertation, Paris: Ecole Nationale de la Statistique et de
   l'Administration Economique.
Corpus Juris Canonici (1879–81), Leipzig: B. Tauchnitz, (2 vols).
Decret, in *Corpus Juris Canonici*, vol.l, *supra*.
Decretals, in *Corpus Juris Canonici*, vol.2, *supra*.
De Roover, R. (1971), *La Pensée economique des scolastiques*, Montréal/Paris: Vrin.
Digest, in *Corpus Juris Civilis*, vol.l, (1968) Dublin/Zürich: Weidmann.
Dumas, A. (1953), Intérêt et usure, in Naz, R. (ed.), *Dictionnaire de droit canonique*, vol.V, Paris:
   Letouzey et Ané.
Giles of Lessines, *De Usuris*, in Thomas Aquinas, *Opera Omnia*, vol.28, Mare, P. and Frette, S.E.
   (eds), (1871–80), Paris: Vivès.
Gordon, B. (1975), *Economic Analysis Before Adam Smith*, London: Macmillan.
Hamelin, A.-M. (ed.) (1962), *Un Traité de morale économique au XIVème siècle*, Louvain/
   Montréal/Lille: Nauwelaerts/Librairie Franciscaine/Giard.
John Duns Scotus, *In Quattuor Libros Sententiarum*, op. oxoniensis, in *Opera Omnia*, (1891–5)
   vol.18 (ed. Wadding, 1639), Paris: Vivès.
Keynes, J.M. (1973), *General Theory of Unemployment, Interest and Money*, in *Collected
   Writings*, vol.7, London: Royal Economic Society.
Langholm, O. (1984), *The Aristotelian Analysis of Usury*, Bergen/Oslo: Universitetsforlaget.
Lapidus, A. (1986), *Le Détour de valeur*, Paris: Economica.
Lapidus, A. (1987), 'La Propriété de la Monnaie: doctrine de l'usure et théorie de l'intérêt',
   Revue économique, **38**(6), Nov.
Le Bras, G. (1950), 'La Doctrine ecclésiastique de l'usure à l'époque classique (XIIème-XIVème
   siècles)', in Vacant, A., Mangenot, E., Amann, E. (eds), *Dictionnaire de théologie catholique*,
   vol.XV(2), Paris: Letouzey et Ané.
McLaughlin, T. P. (1939), 'The Teaching of the Canonists on Usury (XIIth, XIIIth and XIVth
   centuries)', Part 1, *Medieval Studies*, I.
Mélitz, J. (1971), 'Some Further Reassessment of the Scholastic Doctrine of Usury', *Kyklos*, 24.
Nelson, B. (1949), *The Idea of Usury, From Tribal Brotherhood to Universal Otherhood*,
   Princeton: Princeton University Press.
Noonan, J. T. Jr (1957), *The Scholastic Analysis of Usury*, Cambridge (Mass.): Harvard
   University Press.
Raymond of Peñaforte (1744), *Summa de Casibus Conscientiae*, Verona: Augustinum
   Carattonium.
Robert of Courçon, *De Usura*, in Lefevre, G. (ed) (1902), *Le Traité 'De Uusura' de Robert de
   Courçon*, Travaux et Mémoires de l'Université de Lille, vol.10, m.30.
Schumpeter, J. A. (1954), *History of Economic Analysis*, London: Allen and Unwin.
Sommerville, H. (1931), 'Interest and Usury in a New Light', *Economic Journal*, **41**, Dec.
Spicq, C. (1935), 'Appendice II: Renseignements Techniques', in Thomas Aquinas, *Somme
   Théologique, Traité de la Justice*, vol.3, Paris: Editions de la Revue des Jeunes.
Thomas Aquinas (1871–80), *Opera Omnia*, Mare, P. and Frette, S.E. (eds), Paris: Vivès.
Thomas Aquinas, De Malo, in *Opera Omnia*, vol.13, *supra*.
Thomas Aquinas, In Decem Libros Ethicorum ad Nichomachum, in *Opera Omnia*, vol.25, *supra*.
Thomas Aquinas, Summa Theologica, in *Opera Omnia*, vol.3, *supra*.
Viner, J. (1978), 'Religious Thought and Economic Society: Four Chapters of an Unfinished
   Work', *History of Political Economy*, **10**(1), Spring.
William of Auxerre (1986), *Summa Aurea*, Paris: CNRS.

3 Understanding ethical individualism and the administrative tradition in pre-eighteenth century political economy

S. Todd Lowry

Introduction

It is tempting to accept the convenient assumption that individualism, rationality and a socially responsible level of conduct are natural attributes of the average member of a society. However, such an assumption was not only foreign to most social theorists before the Enlightenment, but an examination of its lineage suggests that it has a heavy ideological component.

Individual decision-making, which requires authority and promotes a concern for the moral status and effectiveness of the individual's decisions, grew out of interest in and respect for leadership positions in antiquity. In addition, the effectiveness of the kind of individual who gained status as leader and administrator was traditionally related to personal charisma and individual reputation. The character of the educational tradition of antiquity reflected the training of the élite to be outstanding individuals by emulating heroes of the past. This is, for example, the tenor of Xenophon's *Cyropaedia* which uses the training of Cyrus the Great as an object lesson for would-be leaders. It is more formally illustrated by the more directly designated educational purpose behind Plutarch's collection of biographies of famous leaders which was conspicuous in the European educational tradition into the nineteenth century. The point is that individualism and the refined exercise of responsible choice and leadership have been the prerogative of the élite throughout ancient, medieval and early modern times. The naturalistic democratization or inversion of the pyramid of rational and ethical individualism appears to be a rather recent phenomenon suggesting the need for some ideological analysis as well as an historical overview.

Although at first glance it may seem to be an overly extensive excursion into the past, the Greek and Roman tradition of special status for the patriarchal head of the agrarian estate was of lasting significance. It supported the tradition of a benevolent manor lord that characterized an élitist view of the primarily agrarian economy clear up to Adam Smith's *Theory of Moral Sentiments*. It was reinforced by Platonic philosophy which idealized an élite individualism and supported the tradition of advice literature that was the vector of a nascent political economy up to modern times. It is this background that we must survey as a foundation for examining the ideological component of modern premises of rational individualism in social theory.

From head of the family to efficient administrator

The earliest proto-economic social tradition in our Greco-Roman heritage was a performance mandate imposed upon the patriarch, or head of the extended family in the Mediterranean world (Adkins,1960). The ancient pattern, in both Aryan and Semitic cultures, of aggregating the extended family over three and four generations into a social unit under the control of a patriarchal head, created the setting for a leadership and decision-making tradition. The patriarch had authority over the family members, extending to judicial power of life or death in the case of the Roman 'pater familias' and in some Semitic cultures into modern times. This authority was balanced by a heavy burden to successfully defend and provide for one's 'people'. This success ethic easily developed into an efficiency ethic involving a commitment to agricultural and military planning where fortifications were frequently as important as food in the seasonal struggle for survival. Ulysses, as a culture hero, is an interesting case in point. According to tradition, his shrewdness and rationality illustrated a success or effectiveness standard that accepted and even lauded various levels of deceit and conniving. This emphasis upon the individual as authority figure with a do or die standard for his success is what characterizes the ancient notion of administrative ethics. The tribal head, the shepherd king or emperor ruling over irrigated valleys and the head of the city state all carried this burden of self-interested obligation to manage successfully the social, economic, political and defence needs of their holdings or their community, the old 'bottom line'.

Classical Platonism: noblesse oblige

Plato's writings are seldom examined from the perspective of their influence on political economy as an administrative science. Nevertheless, they include some of the basic foundation-stones of the administrative tradition and élitist political thought. First, running on the theory that no one would voluntarily do anything inconsistent with his own success and well-being, Plato demonstrated that those in authority, no less than any other individual, only err through ignorance. Given correct information and insight, everyone would choose the *best* path toward the achievement of the *best* end. Not only would an individual in authority desire to have the best advice and best information, but those subject to that authority would desire that authority be exercised by the most intelligent and best informed individual possible. Plato characterized political and economic leadership as a matter of technical expertise, and as such, subject to professional self-regulation. As M. I. Findley pointed out in his criticism of

Plato's captain-and-ship analogy in *The Republic* (VI, 488), while the captain should be allowed to run the ship, the passengers might like to have some choice in deciding where they wanted to go (Finley, 1968, p. 88). For Plato, however, this was not a problem. Rational efficiency was implicit in intelligent informed choice and the approach to the preferred or ideal was a function of that rational efficient process. There could be only one end and that was implicit in the rational and efficient management of the state by the best and wisest leaders who could determine the proper ends.

Here is the idealization of the rational individual in its true sense. This is not the average man, the representative of the 'demos' or mob, but the élite individual. How did this individual achieve *rationality* and from whence came his *ethics*?

Rationality

Plato's views on rationality were apparently influenced by philosophers such as Parmenedes and Pythagoras. To them, the *universe*, the oneness of things, offered a totally coherent world subject to deductive analysis. Mathematics was the science of systematic relationships. It abstracted the essence of this coherent universe. Rationality, consistent with its derivation, meant that ideas or relationships were expressible in whole number *ratios* that could therefore be formulated and defined in terms consistent with all other numerical for-mulations. This was extended to the geometrical as well. One of the enduring indicators of this notion of ideal rationality was the premise that if all geometric figures were rational, they could be defined in terms of one another, therefore, a circle of a given area could be defined in terms of a square with the same area from the dimensions of that circle, or vice versa, using only compass and straight edge. This was the persisting problem of 'the squaring of the circle' that occupied Hobbes in his old age.

Once we appreciate this concept of a rationality that is part of a seamless universal fabric, we can appreciate the concept of a single rationality that the intellectually superior individual with some insight resulting from purity of soul, can tune in on. Plato's rational idea of *form* with 'God, The Great Geo-meter' is one of the earliest suggestions of a rational system controlled by an invisible hand. We can also understand how some naturalistic and democratic thinkers could believe that this universal rationality might 'well up' in the consensus of the masses from time to time – *Vox Populi, Vox Dei*, or 'the voice of the people is the voice of God', as Roman writers formulated it.

Ethics

By definition, ethics is an element in voluntary choice. The poor or the subservient do what is required of them and because their activities do not require choice, they are not considered virtuous. People buffeted by the harsh reality of daily subsistence merely respond or fail to survive. Those subject to duty to a superior in a military system or a social hierarchy are expected to serve and to perform. Public virtue involves the capacity to make intelligent effective choices in public affairs. The element of choice thus supports the concept of excellence and effectiveness or efficient administration.

But why would an individual choose to act in the public interest when his own private interest might be advanced at the public expense? The Egyptian Pharaoh, for example, lived in a duty hierarchy in which he served as a steward on earth for his deified father who looked down from heaven, judging his actions. He had to look forward to being judged or evaluated upon his death. The Hebrews absorbed much of this duty morality (Brandon, 1967). In a Greek or Roman city state, this tradition of stewardship and duty did not fit into the religious tradition. Men were virtuous or excellent out of pride in their own competence and desire for the respect and admiration of their peers. Success was its own reward, however, and there were, from time to time, instances of cheating in the Olympic games. Plato pointed out in Book II of the *Republic* that the exceptionally capable individual could fool the populace and manipulate them to his own selfish ends. The issue was clearly faced: an open political system, parallel to an open market system with a free play of ideas and information, could be manipulated to private advantage by the exceptional individual. Although individuals with access to political power could be counted upon to choose actions reflecting their own self-interest, the self-interest of the intelligent individual lay in developing a stable and well ordered mind and body. His prime commitment was to see that his own inner self was *just* or well ordered. Excellence and efficiency in personal behaviour, as a voluntary objective, coincided with offering one's services to provide leadership for the state toward a just (well ordered) and efficient (successful) society. The guideline for this system of ethical or personal choices was rationality, that is, that same rationality that described the orderly universe and that could be sketched in mathematical terms.

What we have here is an intellectual tradition that does a number of things that can be recognized in both pre-eighteenth century social thought and in post-eighteenth century social theory as well. First, the macrocosm has only one rational order and proper fitting into the macrocosmic system, whether it be social or physical, requires an adjustment to the truths and laws that are revealed through mathematics. Second, the microcosm of the individual psyche is striving to stay in tune with the macrocosmic order. The outstanding leader has no other objective than to maximize his own internal rationality by maintaining due ratio and proportion and simultaneously interacting with the macrocosmic rational order. If such an individual deviates from the optimum path, it is only through ignorance and he will gladly accept instruction since his self-improvement is to his own advantage, and his self-interest coincides with the rational interests of the cosmos, or any given part of it such as family, city, state, or even a market. Adam Smith used the term 'benevolence' when referring to this aspect of individual virtue in his *Theory of Moral Sentiments.* Third, things would work better if the average person would do his duty unquestioningly and leave leadership to those trained to make informed choices. There being only one rational optimum, efficiency is a matter of technical expertise and the proven leader or manager is best equipped to lead to the one and only true rational end. Lastly, what evolved out of this reenforcement of the right and duty of the aristocracy to rule was a merging of the concept of rationality both with religion and with natural law theory. Religion, resting on the divinely ordained rational cosmos, endorsed the divine right of kings and scholastic rationality. Naturalism, assuming an interdependence and consistency of all ongoing processes in the cosmos, accepted rational elaboration as the avenue for understanding natural truth and natural law.

Although rationality was recognized as the fabric of reality, the social phase of the rational fabric left room for irrational departures from correct lines of choice. The critical difference in the exercise of choice based upon understanding required attention to be directed primarily to the human variable. For that reason, the classic works that can be characterized as the political economy of the pre-eighteenth century take the form of advice on how to be an effective leader. Xenophon summed up the lore of his day in the fourth century BC with his *Oeconomicus* and his oft quoted *Poroi* or *Ways and Means.* This latter tract on how to increase the revenues of Athens was still considered pertinent enough to be included as an appendix to late-seventeenth and early-eighteenth-century editions of Davenant and Petty (Lowry, 1987, p. 49). An absence of a proper appreciation of this genre by historians of economic ideas is one of the 'blind spots' in the history of the discipline. It was the dominant form of political writing up to modern times and carried the accumulated knowledge of public administration, taxation, and monetary policy as part of political science. These tracts, called *Specula* or *Mirrors for Princes*, deserve systematic attention as representations of the science of economic administration.

The Mirror for Princes and Wisdom Literature

This form of literature dates from the very earliest times. There are classic pieces from early Egyptian writings in the form of letters of advice from a father or wise friend to a future ruler. They are educational tracts written in a vivid applied setting which, perhaps, was their actual origin. Hesiod's well known *Works and Days* parallels this pattern being a letter of advice to a wayward brother. This assumption, that 'a word to the wise (or rational) should be sufficient,' had very ancient roots.

The term 'mirror for princes' comes into north European literature with the famous *Secretum Secretorum (Kitâb sirr al-asrâr)* (The Book of Secrets), or 'The Letter to Alexander', that was allegedly written by Aristotle advising his ex-pupil (Manzalaoui, 1977). This document gave rise to over five hundred Latin manuscript copies dating back to the twelfth century AD. Its Arabic original, dating from perhaps the eighth century AD had as its primary title *The Book of the Science of Government On the Good Ordering of Statecraft.* This is about as close a paraphrase of the concept of political economy as one could expect from a writer who was unfamiliar with the subsequent terminology. Latin translations derive from Spanish and Palestinian (Crusades period) sources and the first complete English version dates from the mid fifteenth century.

What is most striking about 'The Letter to Alexander' is the attention it placed on the anthropocentric element. In discussing trade and taxation, it emphasized utilitarian responses to policy. In discussing effective leadership and administration, it placed such extensive and detailed emphasis on the importance of the maintenance of good health by the ruler that it received primary attention as a medical tract from such early scholars as Roger Bacon. On the administrative side, we are reminded that a secretary is the keeper of an executive's innermost secrets and should be chosen with extreme care and well rewarded. It also gave extensive phrenological data to aid in the evaluation and selection of personnel for various roles. Interest in this latter aspect of the work has distracted scholars from its basic scientific approach to administration. It even contained an eminently useful suggestion for today's chief executive officer, or political leader, worthy of Tom Peters or Ross Perot. The suggestion is to have an informal party with your major personnel several times a year, and see to it that the liquor flows freely so that they all get drunk, while you yourself, remain clear headed. It is suggested that a great deal of valuable administrative insight can be gathered from such an exercise!

In the same anthropocentric tradition, we find the much better known book directed to the 'Magnificent Lorenzo de Medichi' by Niccolo Machiavelli written *c.* 1513. In asserting 'my readiness to serve you,' he went on, 'I have not found anything I prize so much or value so highly as my knowledge of the actions of men, acquired through long experience of contemporary affairs and extended reading in those of antiquity' (Machiavelli, 1513, p. 3).

We find a similar though less professional expression of this same tradition in Erasmus's *The Education of a Christian Prince* of 1518. This long instructional guide on personal morality and proper conduct for a responsible ruler–administrator was directed to the young prince who later became Emperor Charles V of Spain.

A more interesting though diffuse work was the widely distributed and reprinted *Mirror for Magistrates* of 1559 (Campbell, 1938). This collection of leadership experiences from English history was promoted as examples or a 'mirror' from history by which the trials and travails of figures from the past could be studied. In this case, they were primarily examples of what not to do and how not to behave when in positions of authority. It is also of interest because it gave a hint of the democratization or popularization of the administrative and aristocratic individualist tradition. These examples are potentially instructive for lesser beings as well as for the nobility, carrying their special burden of leadership in the Platonist tradition.

The general popularization of Renaissance learning was characteristic of the sixteenth century and the emerging merchant class was beginning to assert pride of class and embrace formal learning (Collins, 1989, pp. 128–34). This process presaged the wide distribution of economic and policy tracts during the seventeenth century which were beginning to reflect the naturalistic rejection of sovereign administrative authority in favour of a popular individualism. The legal maxim, for example, that a man's home is his castle is more than just a borrowing of the moral force of feudal prerogative. It is a popular inversion of the premises that gave special status to the manor lord in his castle *vis-à-vis* the sovereign authority of the king.

Meanwhile, the principles of administrative efficiency that were consistent with a rational cosmic order only partially died out. They were replaced with attempts to justify the diffusion of administrative authority over the economy to large numbers of individuals who shared in ultimate rationality. Gerard Malynes, in 1623, specifically rejected the premise that the gain-oriented merchant would necessarily maximize the public interest through his individual rationality. On empirical grounds he found individuals fallible. However, he perpetuated the administrative assumption that a sovereign could and should regulate to the advantage of the public interest, a view developed into a political imperative by Thomas Hobbes in the mid seventeenth century.

The ideological need to justify Platonic rationality in the hands of the practising merchant class proved too strong. By Adam Smith's time, we see a theory in which practising merchants, through the natural imperative of a competitive market process, express approximations of ideal rational behaviour in the market place. The complexities and inversions of democratic and élitist ideas in this period are difficult to disentangle. Clear and quite challenging, however, is the almost complete failure to recall or face Plato's point that an open popular participative politics would result in manipulative control by the very élite that such openness was designed to eliminate. In particular, the transference of this theory from the political to the market forum had no ideological appeal. The end result by 1776 was a theory of an open individualistic economy, administered by an 'invisible hand,' that guaranteed the public interest supported by an inherent natural rationality.

Intuition and informed rational analysis by the élite administrator ceased to characterize political–economic thinking. The merchant–manufacturer was left to follow his natural drive for gain and the buffeting of the market kept him boxed into a naturally rational adjustment as long as he could exercise primitive economic reflexes. However, the individualistic emphasis on the creative or productive importance of the élite decision-maker seems to have persisted in a dual form. In part, it survived by identifying the creator of wealth in a democratized form, that is, as the labour theory of value, thus attributing value to the efforts of all individuals, not to nature. At the same time, the élite tradition of administrative expertise and efficiency survived as an emphasis upon entrepreneurship. In a real sense, the modern mystique surrounding entrepreneurs with all their ideological reinforcement and special pleading is the reincarnation of the Platonic administrator and the feudal grandee wearing his halo at a jaunty angle and bearing the burden of *noblesse oblige* with just a hint of smugness.

References

Adkins, A. W. H. (1960), *Merit and Responsibility: A Study in Greek Values*, Oxford: Clarendon Press.

Appleby, J. O. (1978), *Economic Thought and Ideology in Seventeenth-Century England*, Princeton: Princeton University Press.

Brandon, S. G. F. (1967), *The Judgment of the Dead: The Idea of Life After Death in the Major Religions*, New York: Scribner's.

Campbell, L. B. (ed.) (1938), *The Mirror for Magistrates*, (first published 1559) Cambridge: Cambridge University Press.

Collins, S. L. (1989), *From Divine Cosmos to Sovereign State: An Intellectual History of Consciousness and the Idea of Order in Renaissance England*, Oxford: Oxford University Press.

Erasmus, D. (1515), *The Education of a Christian Prince*, trans. with intro. by L. K. Born, (1936), New York: Columbia University Press.

Finley, M. I. (1968) *Aspects of Antiquity: Discoveries and Controversies*, New York: Viking Press.

Hesiod (1959), *Hesiod*, trans. by R. Lattimore, Ann Arbor, Michigan: University of Michigan Press.

Lowry, S. T. (1987), *The Archaeology of Economic Ideas*, Durham, N.C: Duke University Press.

Machiavelli, N. (1513), *The Prince*, trans. by R. M. Adams, (1977), New York: W. W. Norton & Company, Inc.

Manzalaoui, M. A. (ed.) (1977), *Secretum Secretorum*, nine English versions, vol. I, texts, published for The Early English Text Society, Oxford: Oxford University Press.

Plato (1963), 'The Republic' in E. Hamilton and H. Cairnes (eds), *The Collected Dialogues of Plato*, Princeton: Princeton University Press.

Smith, A. (1813), *The Theory of Moral Sentiments*, 1759 (2 vols), Edinburgh: J. Hay.

Xenophon (1918–68), *Xenophon* (Works), Loeb Classical Library, nos 51–2, 83–90, 168, Cambridge, Mass.: Harvard University Press; London: W. Heinemann.

PART II

VARIATIONS ON CLASSICAL THEMES

4 John Law: aspects of his monetary and debt management policies

Antoin E. Murphy[1]

Introduction

In 1705 John Law published *Money and Trade Consider'd; with a Proposal for Supplying the Nation with Money* (Edinburgh), which recommended to the Scottish Parliament the establishment of a land bank in Scotland. For a short period his proposal, along with a competing one from Hugh Chamberlen, engaged the attention of the parliamentarians, even provoking two members to meet on Leith strand, outside Edinburgh, to duel over it. The Parliament was however more interested in discussing the prospects of union with England, with the result that monetary issues were soon forgotten.

Money and Trade re-appeared at two significant points of time in the eighteenth century. In 1720 it was translated and published in French, and two further editions, with London imprints, were published in English. In 1790 it was published again in French, in a collection of works edited by de Sénovert. In both 1720 and 1790 France was involved in major macroecononic experiments involving monetary and debt management policy. In 1720, Law, by then the Controller General of Finances, and virtual prime minister of France, was very much the catalyst behind a dramatic transformation in French economic policy; in 1790 France was embarking on the creation of a new type of money, the assignats, issued against the collateral of confiscated Church property and lands, and therefore similar in outline to Law's earlier proposals for a land bank. Opponents of the assignats scheme found it convenient to link Law's failed economic experiment to the assignats. Advocates of the assignats found it necessary to distinguish between Law's System, which they dismissed as a chimera produced by a Scottish charlatan, and the assignats, which they maintained were substantively different from Law's paper money. In brief, Law found no friends amongst the revolutionaries, receiving a distinctly bad press from both sides.

This antipathy towards Law during the French Revolution has a modern parallel in the distrust and neglect modern economists have also shown towards him. Keynes never referred to Law in *The General Theory* – he mentioned him once in *A Treatise on Money* – though Law had embarked on the major 'Keynesian' experiment of the eighteenth century. Monetarists, while happy to find intellectual lineages with Richard Cantillon and David Hume, have steered away from Law, probably feeling that he is of little interest given his well known views on the merits of monetary expansion.

Yet, Law was the first economist to use the term *the demand for money*, so crucial to the formulation of the quantity theory of money. He was also the first economist to put forward the law of one price for internationally traded goods, a key concept in the monetary approach to the balance of payments. Correctly, in my view, Schumpeter ranks Law as one of the outstanding monetary theorists, not just of the eighteenth century, but of 'all times' (Schumpeter, 1954, p. 295).

Law's writings

The first attempt to publish Law's economic writings in a collected form was appropriately made in 1790 when Law's name was being cited so frequently in the French Assembly. The work *Oeuvres...de John Law, contenant les principes sur le numéraire, le commerce, le credit et les banques* was edited by General Etienne de Sénovert (de Sénovert, 1790).

It was not till 1934, however, that a more comprehensive edition of Law's writings, *Oeuvres complètes de John Law*, was published in three volumes under the editorship of Paul Harsin (Harsin,1934). Care needs to be exercised in using them as the basic text for analysing Law's ideas. The extensive article 'Restablissement du commerce' which occupies two thirds of Volume 2 has now been conclusively shown to have been written by Pottier de La Hestroye rather than by Law. Doubts also arise as to the authorship of a number of other pieces including the 'Idée générale du nouveau système des finances' and the 'Lettre ecrite à M. ... sur le nouveau système des finances'. These caveats aside, Harsin's work is most valuable in that it helps us to understand the evolution of Law's ideas after the publication of *Money and Trade* in 1705.

Law's background

Law, born in 1671 in Edinburgh, was very much a product of his background and his age. His father was a prominent Edinburgh goldsmith at a time when goldsmiths doubled as rudimentary bankers. Law acquired the banking gene from his father, but, ironically, he eschewed the use of gold either as money, or as the appropriate asset backing for money. His rejection of gold may be seen in the context of the age he lived in, for with the growth in colonial trade and the concomitant enlargement of public sector debt, caused by frequent wars, there was a widespread growth of new financial instruments. The establishment of the Bank of England in 1694, the expansion of the East India Company in the first decade of the eighteenth century, and the creation of the South Sea Company in 1711 provided the base for the emergence of financial capitalism in England. Law, as will be shown, was greatly influenced by the English models.

Money and trade

Law's first known economic work, *Money and Trade Consider'd; with a Proposal for Supplying the Nation with Money* (Edinburgh,1705) dealt with the economic problems of Scotland rather than England. Having acquired a reputation as a rake as well as a gambler, and a capital conviction for killing a rival in a duel in London, Law escaped from the prison where he was incarcerated and re-appeared in his native town of Edinburgh in 1705. There he advanced his proposals to the Scottish Parliament for the establishment of a land bank in Scotland. There was nothing original in the proposal for a land bank – there had been a number of similar proposals over the previous decade by writers such as Barbon, Briscoe and Chamberlen. Law's originality lay in the theory which he presented to back up his policy recomendations. This theory transcended the usual type of crude economic writing to be found in the pamphlet literature of the period.

Law was the first in a line of distinguished eighteenth century writers, a group which included Cantillon, Hume and Quesnay, to develop a macroeconomic vision of economic processes. Throughout his career he worried about the lack of employment opportunities and the underutilization of resources in economies such as those of Scotland and France.

The cause of these problems was identified by Law as being due to a shortage of money accompanied by excessively high interest rates. Money and trade, as the title of his work indicated, were linked together. Money, in his opinion, drove trade. Trade can be taken as a synonym for what is referred to, in modern terminology, as economic activity. He showed that barter was inefficient because it either stopped or delayed mutually beneficial trades. Once a financial instrument evolved as money, economic activity increased. He implied that if the use of money could raise economic activity above the level prevailing at the barter state, then increases in the money supply could push the economy to a higher level of activity in which all resources were better utilized:

> As money increased, the disadvantages and inconveniencies of barter were removed; the poor and idle were employed, more of the land was laboured, the product increased, manufactures and trade improved, the landed men lived better, and the people with less dependance on them (I, 14).

Law believed that by increasing the money supply it was possible to increase economic activity, which, in turn, would increase the demand for money, thereby locking the increased money supply into the domestic economy without inflationary or balance of payments effects. To Law the demand for money was 'proportion'd to people, land or product', with product being synonymous with what is defined as national income today. The juxtaposition of people and land with (national) product takes on a greater meaning later, for Law's concept of the optimum quantity of money involved a fully employed economy where people and land were fully utilized:

> It cannot well be known what sum will serve the occasions of the nation, for as manufacture and trade advance, *the demand for money* will increase; but the many poor we have always had, is a great presumption we have never had money enough (I,158), (my emphasis).

Starting with a disequilibrium situation of unemployment, Law believed that each increase in the money supply would, by generating an increase in economic activity and employment, thereby create an increase in the demand for money:

> The paper money proposed being always equal in quantity to the demand, the people will be employed, the country improved, manufacture advanced, trade domestic and foreign will be carried on, and wealth and power attained (I,139).

Law thus implicitly assumed that there was a potential demand for money up to that level of economic activity consistent with full employment. Like a latter day monetarist he realized that if the money supply was expanded out of line with the demand for money it would have inflationary repercussions:

> If money were given to a people in greater quantity than there was a demand for, money would fall in its value; but if only given equal to the demand it will not fall in value (I,160).

When discussing the inflationary repercussions arising from an overexpansion of the money supply Law introduced an important *caveat* by making allowances for what is now termed the law of one price for internationally traded goods. Law emphasized that prices in a small open economy are determined by international prices rather than by domestic money supply factors. William Petyt in *Brittania Languens* (1680) had argued that prices are proportionately related to the money supply. In strikingly pre-Humean language, Petyt had asked what would have happened if the English money supply had been reduced to only £500. Would this not have caused oxen to be sold for a penny each? Law disagreed, contending that as oxen were internationally traded goods their price would be determined by international rather than by domestic factors. As oxen could be exported their price would be determined by that potentially available on markets, such as the neighbouring Dutch market, rather than in a depressed English market.

Monetary policy and debt management

There is an important distinction to be made between Scotland, as depicted in *Money and Trade* in 1705 and France between 1716 and 1720 when Law's star was in its ascendancy. Scotland, like France, faced a *monetary crisis* caused, in Law's view, by a shortage of money and high interest rates. France had the additional complication of a *financial crisis* in the form of a high level of state indebtedness.

While many commentators can understand, and in some cases identify with, Law's recommendation for the establishment of a bank, they cannot understand why Law attempted to push his policies further than this by constructing the complex structure that later came to be known as the Mississippi System. These views do not, in my opinion, recognize the way in which Law's economic thought evolved between his writing of *Money and Trade* and the acceptance by the Regent of his banking proposal in 1716. The evolution of Law's thought was greatly influenced by first, the pace and success of financial innovation in England and second, the realization that the French financial structure, in which his monetary policies were to operate, was quite different than that which had prevailed in Scotland in 1705. These factors forced Law to embark on a far more grandiose and complex system than that outlined in *Money and Trade*.

It must be remembered that at the time of writing *Money and Trade* the Bank of England was just ten years old and still a comparatively weak institution. A land bank proposal had actually been legislated by Parliament in the late 1690s which potentially could have produced a strong competitive opposition to the Bank. Furthermore the Bank was still not immune from bank runs and it had no long term charter for its activities. It was very much at an embryonic and growing stage of its career. Over the next decade, between 1705 and 1715, the Bank grew in stature and influence, a growth that Law was careful to analyse.

In *Money and Trade* Law had recommended the creation of a paper money collateralized by land. The envisaged bank would have had the following balance sheet:

Proposed Land Bank

Assets	*Liabilities*
Land	Banknotes

The Bank of England had, however, succeeded in issuing banknotes – not against the collateral of land – but against the collateral of specie reserves, government securities, and, to a limited extent, loans to the private sector. Its basic balance sheet consisted of:

Bank of England

Assets	Liabilities
Specie reserves	Shares
Government securities	Banknotes
Loans to private sector	

This type of emerging bank interested Law in that it was acting not just as a *deposit taking* institution, such as the Bank of Amsterdam, but as a *credit creating* institution, lending the bulk of its funds, at this time, to the state. The Bank was increasing the money supply in England, something he had stated, in *Money and Trade*, was necessary for the English economy. There were further important developments arising from the Bank's activities, first, government securities could form part of the asset backing of the bank; and second, shares of the Bank had many of the characteristics of a medium of exchange and were being exchanged as a new type of money by merchants in London.

Other financial innovations further influenced Law's evolving thought. Chief of these were the continuing growth of the East India Company and the establishment of the South Sea Company. Both of these institutions were trading companies which undertook to lend money to the government in return for monopoly privileges over certain sectors of the colonial trade. The basic balance sheet of these companies was as follows:

East India and South Sea Companies

Assets	Liabilities
Monopoly trading privileges	Shares
Working capital	
Government securities	

As Law felt that the shares of the Bank of England acted as a type of money, he also accepted that the shares of the East India and South Sea companies had similar liquidity attributes. In the 'Memoire pour prouver qu'une nouvelle espèce de monnaie peut être meilleure que l'or et l'argent', written in 1707, Law remarked: 'These shares [of the East India Company] are not promises of payment in specie, they are a new type of money' (I, 205). He went on to explain in the *mémoire* that the shares of the East India Company were different from other types of money, in that part of the asset backing of the Company was not specie but productive capital in the form of trading ships and forts, inventories of merchandise, and so on. Thus in Law's vision of the monetary system there were other assets that could be more usefully utilized as backing for money than gold or silver specie.

Law therefore interpreted paper money and shares as having liquidity characteristics which made them useful media of exchange – he did not give enough attention to the possibility of share prices falling; indeed he felt that their asset backing was such as to make them stores of value. Here, in my opinion, we find Law advancing a very modernistic conception of money. To him money could be defined in terms of the liquidity characteristics of financial instruments rather than in narrow terms of just specie.

In a forthcoming paper in the *European Economic Review*, I have attempted to show that even prior to the establishment of the General Bank, Law had conceptualized the essential elements of what I have categorized as his grand design ('The Evolution of John Law's Monetary Theory 1707–1715'). Fear of being dismissed as an idealistic visionary led him to be circumspect in disclosing details of this grand design in his *mémoires* recommending the establishment of a General Bank. However, there are glimpses in comments made in the 'Lettre au Régent' when Law remarked 'I had the honour to tell him [the Regent] then that my idea for a bank was not my biggest, that I had one by which I would furnish 500 millions which would cost the public nothing' (II, 265).

Law had been forced to think in terms of the grand design because France faced not just the problem of a shortage of money but also, the additional complicating burden of a very high level of national debt that had been accumulated through the bellicosity and profligacy of Louis XIV. Law had to find a way to expand the money supply and at the same time to control the national debt. If he was to lower the interest rate, Law had to involve himself not only with monetary policy but also with debt management operations. The structure of the French financial system dictated that he thought in wider terms than a limited expansion of banknotes issued through the General Bank.

The English models which he had examined served as an inspiration. The Bank of England combined monetary expansion, through its creation of shares and banknotes, with debt management operations, through its uptake of government securities. Furthermore, shares issued by the trading companies increased liquidity in the economy and at the same time helped fund the government's borrowing requirement.

Law's General Bank, established in May 1716, was modelled on the Bank of England in that it obtained its banking privileges in return for taking up part of the national debt – in its case, part of the outstanding amount of *billets d'état*. The Company of the West (Compagnie d'Occident), founded in August 1717, which was given monopoly trading rights over Louisiana – an area representing half of the land mass of the United States today (excluding Alaska) – had close parallels with the East India and South Sea Companies. It acquired the trading rights to Louisiana in return for restructuring, and accepting a lower interest rate, on part of the outstanding amount of *billets d'état*. The company benefitted in that it acquired rights to exploit the agricultural and mineral potential of this huge area. The state benefitted in that part of its floating short term debt was converted into long term debt which bore a lower rate of interest. Shareholders, in the new company, who swapped *billets d'état* in return for the company's shares, had the prospect of large capital gains if the wealth of Louisiana was properly exploited.

Law went on to use the Company of the West to mount a series of spectacular takeovers and mergers while, at the same time, greatly developing the General Bank by ensuring that it was used as the government's bank for the receipt and disbursement of state funds. In August 1718 the Company of the West acquired the lease of the tobacco farm, while in December it took over the Company of Senegal. In the same month the General Bank's operations were reorganized and it was re-named the Royal Bank, a development that showed the extent to which Law had become a key member of the Regent's inner circle. In May 1719 Law merged the enlarged Company of the West with the Company of the East Indies and China to form what was termed the Company of the Indies. Further acquisitions in the form of the Company of Africa and the lease of the Mint were made in June and July of that year. These acquisitions and mergers required financing which Law arranged through the issue of three tranches of shares known as the *mères, filles*, and *petites filles*. The *mères*, issued in 1717 on the establishment of the Company of the West, were subscribed for in *billets d'état*, which were standing at a very sizeable discount. Effectively they cost around 150 livres in 1717, though issued at a nominal price of 500 livres. The *filles* were issued in June 1719 at 550 livres, a 50 livres premium suggesting wider public interest in the shares after an interval of nearly two years. The share price jumped in July enabling Law to issue a further batch of shares, this time at 1000 livres each. By the end of July 1719 Law's Company had issued 300 000 shares with a nominal value of 150 million livres, which would have cost transactors, assuming the 70 per cent discount on *billets d'état* in 1717/18, around 108 million livres.

The share price having jumped from 500 to over 1000 in July 1719 the stage was set for Europe's first major stock market boom. This boom was linked to Law's wish to take over completely France's national debt by swapping shares for government securities. The sheer magnitude of this operation proved to be breathtaking.

On 26 August 1719 the Regent presented Law's proposal for the Mississippi Company, as it was popularly known, to take over the tax farms and the remainder of the national debt. This project had been examined, according to the Duc D'Antin, by the Regent for 'a long time'. It was not, in other words, a sudden flash of inspiration by Law but rather represented a crucial part of a long thought out strategy.

Retrospectively in the 'Histoire des Finances' Law commented that, despite the success of his operations up to the middle of July 1719, they had not cured the most 'profound wounds' of the state. 'What had been seen so far was more in the form of a preparation for the cure than a radical cure. . .' (III,344). Later on in this work he remarked, 'The object of the System did not stop with the establishment of a moderate credit ... this would have sufficed in a state with a small debt burden' (III,378). A far more ambitious plan was called for. Law's plan, unveiled on 26 August, was to lend the King 1.2 billion livres at an interest rate of 3 per cent so as to retire the national debt by this amount. While initially the loan was to be raised from the public through the sale of a type of company bond paying a 3 per cent rate of interest, Law quickly moved away from this idea to one of raising the money through further issues of shares in the Company. Essentially debt holders were being forced to give up their government debt, on which a 5 per cent rate of interest was paid, while at the same time they were offered the possibility of acquiring shares of the company, yielding far less in terms of dividend but possessing the prospect of sizeable capital gains. With the share price jumping from 2250 on 1 August to 2940 on 14 August, to 5000 and over in mid-September, capital gains rather than dividends occupied the minds of most transactors.

In the space of eight days, between 26 September and 2 October 1719, Law's Company issued 300 000 shares at 5000 livres per share, to be paid in instalments; the total issue of these eight days amounted to 1.5 billion livres, some fourteen times the amount raised by the Company between September 1717 and 1719. Additionally, existing shareholders were sitting on sizeable capital gains, gains which increased as the price of shares rose to over 9000 in late November 1719 and a high of 10 000 on 2 December. At this point the market valuation of the Mississippi Company was 6.24 billion livres. Concomitant with these developments the banknote issue of the Royal Bank had been increased from 160 million livres in June to 1 billion livres by the end of 1719 as money was lent to existing shareholders to purchase further shares.

France was awash with liquidity, particularly after the company guaranteed a floor price of 9000 livres a share in early 1720 through the establishment of a buying and selling agency known as the 'bureau d'achat et de vente'. Effectively, this monetized shares, a development consistent with Law's already written views that they constituted a new type of money.

In February 1720 the Royal Bank and the Company of the Indies were formally merged together. At this juncture, Law, who had been appointed Controller General of Finances in January 1720 wrote, 'One sees here a sequence of ideas which are interlinked and which reveal more and more the principle on which they are based' (III,98–9). For a while the System, in all its unifying beauty, seemed to work. Economic activity boomed, the national debt seemed to be under control, money was plentiful and the interest rate had been driven down to 2 per cent. Unfortunately for Law, there were significant flaws in the system, flaws that Cantillon was quick to notice and exploit, see *Richard Cantillon:Entrepreneur and Economist* (Murphy,1986).

Law had created a financial system the long term viability of which was crucially dependent on the growth of the real economy. There had to be some equilibrium relationship between the financial system and the real economy. For a while a temporary equilibrium existed as transactors seemed content to remain within the financial circuit trading money for shares and shares for money. However, once money started spilling over from the financial circuit into the real economy at too fast a rate, problems arose. The real economy proved to be incapable of generating a sufficient growth in commodities to match the monetary expansion, so that the excess money created inflation and balance of payments problems. Law had believed that the growth in the real economy, spurred on by monetary expansion, would always be sufficient to mop up the newly created money. Indeed he went further and argued in the 'Memoire sur les Banques' (II,6) that monetary expansion would lead to a balance of payments surplus.

For a period Law attempted to force transactors back into the financial circuit by a series of measures ranging from prohibitions on the holding of large amounts of specie, to the demonetization of gold and a phased monthly demonetization of silver. Temporarily these measures worked, as Faure (1977, pp. 376–85) has shown. But there was still too much liquidity in the System. On 21 May 1720 an *arrêt* was promulgated stipulating that shares were to be reduced by four ninths (from 9000 to 5000) and banknotes by a half (for example, a banknote worth 10 000 livres would be reduced to 5000 livres) between May and December. This was an attempt to reduce the liquidity of the System thereby bringing the financial circuit back into line with the real economy. Despite the revocation of the 21 May *arrêt* a couple of days later – due to public pressure – the effect on confidence was so great that the System never recovered from it. The price of shares and banknotes fell continuously during the Summer and Autumn of 1720, and Law was forced to flee the country in December with the aid of the Regent.

Conclusion

With the collapse of the System there were considerable losses over a wide cross-section of the French populace. Debtors for the most part gained at the expense of creditors. The state, the biggest debtor, gained in the short term at the expense of the rentiers through a reduction of its debt. Over the long term, the costs of the System were great because confidence in financial innovation and in paper money had been destroyed. The old structures that Law had dismantled, controlled by the financiers and their noble backers, were restored.

France moved back onto the *ancien regime's* well rutted financial track that would inevitably lead to the Revolution.

Ironically when it came to reforming this financial system in the 1790s, the revolutionaries did not acknowledge how close Law had come to producing a financial revolution. Instead Law's name was dragged through the Assembly's debates as a type of financial ogre whose policies needed to be unequivocally condemned. Yet, the revolutionaries should have recognized that, as was the case during Law's System, France once again faced the dual problems of a shortage of money and a sizeable national debt. The assignats were issued over the short term to meet the shortage of money, and, over the long term, were intended to be used as a method for reducing the national debt. In distancing themselves from Law the revolutionaries missed an opportunity to learn from Law's mistakes. By examining his System they could have learnt about the dangers of over-expanding the money supply and the appropriate parameters within which a limited expansion of the money supply was feasible. Instead the assignats were massively over-issued and France experienced a hyper-inflation which led to a further collapse in confidence in paper money in France.

At the theoretical level Law's System provoked a number of significant contributions to eighteenth century monetary theory. Law himself wrote a number of retrospective *mémoires* attempting to justify its existence. Two of his assistants, Melon (1734) and Dutot (1738,1935), wrote works which were broadly sympathetic to Law's approach. This approach was firmly rejected by the powerful financier Pâris-Duverney (1740), and at an intellectual level contested by Cantillon in his *Essai* (1755).

Notes

1. I wish to acknowledge my appreciation for the assistance I received in researching this chapter from the Benefaction Fund Trinity College Dublin, the Institut National d'Etudes Démographiques in Paris, and the French Ministry of Foreign Affairs.
2. All references to Law's works in the text are taken from *John Law: Oeuvres Complètes* edited in three volumes by Paul Harsin (Paris,1934; re-print Vaduz, 1980).

References

Cantillon, R. (1755), *Essai sur la Nature du Commerce en General*, translated by Henry Higgs (1959), London: Frank Cass and Company.

Daire, E. (ed.) (1843), *Economistes Financiers du XVIIIe Siècle*, Paris: Guillamin.

Dutot, C. (1738), *Réflexions politiques sur les finances et le commerce*, Paris. An extended version of the book was edited by Paul Harsin in 1935.

Faure, E. (1977), *La Banqueroute de Law*, Paris: Gallimard.

Harsin, P. (ed.) (1980), *Oeuvres complètes de John Law*, Paris: Vaduz.

Melon, J.F. (1734), *Essai Politique sur le Commerce*.

Murphy, A. (1986), *Richard Cantillon: Entrepreneur and Economist*, Oxford: Oxford University Press.

Pâris-Duverney, J. (1740), *Examen du livre intitulé refléxions politiques sur les finances et le commerce*, The Hague: V. and N. Prevot.

Petyt, W. (1680), *Brittania Languens*, Reprinted in J.R. McCulloch (ed.) (1856), *Early English Tracts on Commerce*, London: printed for the Political Economy Club.

Schumpeter, J.A. (1954), *History of Economic Analysis*, London: George Allen and Unwin.
De Sénovert, E. (ed.) (1790), *J. Law, Oeuvres...de John Law, contenant les principes sur le numéraire, le commerce, le crédit et les banques*, Paris: Buisson.

5 Moral sentiments and the marketplace: the consistency of *The Theory of Moral Sentiments* and *The Wealth of Nations*

Mary Ann Dimand and Robert W. Dimand[1]

This chapter demonstrates that the commercial co-ordination of *The Wealth of Nations* is consistent with the existence of moral sentiments, and thus shows not only that 'Das Adam Smith Problem' is a myth, but that Toynbee's and Polanyi's assertion of the inhumanity of classical economics does not apply to the economics of Smith. We give the extra assumptions necessary for equilibrium to exist where there are moral sentiments, which has not previously been done, and show that Smith himself made all of these assumptions, with the sole exception of continuity. Further, we show that this equilibrium is Pareto-optimal.

The German historical school found Adam Smith's 1759 *Theory of Moral Sentiments* (TMS) inconsistent with his 1776 *Wealth of Nations* (WN) (Nieli (1986); Teichgraeber (1986)). TMS opens by supposing that

> there are evidently some principles in [man's] nature, which interest him in the fortune of others, and render their happiness necessary to him, though he derives nothing from it [TMS, 1].

The Germans claimed that this analytical framework cannot be reconciled with that of WN, citing particularly the famous passage,

> It is not from the benevolence of the butcher, the brewer, or the baker, that we expect our dinner, but from their regard to their own interest. We address ourselves, not to their humanity but to their self-love, and never talk to them of our own necessities but their advantages [WN, I.ii.2].

Since the two works were not consistent, these German economists claimed, Smith must have changed his mind between publications. Edwin Cannan's 1896 publication of the notes to Smith's 1762 lecture course revealed that the major ideas of WN existed in Smith's lectures on Expediency, while his Ethics lectures still held the ideas codified in TMS (Smith (1982); cf. Nieli (1986)). Furthermore, although Smith revised TMS several times and the last revision was published posthumously in 1792, his revisions simply emphasized pre-existing chapters. The burden of TMS remained unchanged even after the publication of WN. Smith, then, apparently saw no inconsistency between the two works, and certainly he did not change his mind between the publications. August Oncken's name is usually associated with the claim of inconsistency, presumably because of the title of his 1898 *Das Adam Smith-Problem*. Oncken (1897), however, recognizes that the evidence of the lecture notes and Smith's post-1776 revisions militates against the incompatibility of the two works.

A smaller and more recent literature discusses the consistency of TMS and WN. Macfie (1967), Hollander (1973), West (1976), Anspach (1972), and Wilson (1976) note that some important ideas, notably those of laudable self-love and the invisible hand itself, appear in both TMS and WN. Campbell (1967), West (1976), Anspach (1972), and Wilson (1976) argue that the sympathy of TMS gives rise to a political and judicial system which is necessary for the existence of a society of self-interested individuals, while Danner (1976) similarly states that moral sentiments place bounds on the self-interest of WN. Campbell (1967), Viner (1968), and Nieli (1986) make a 'spheres of intimacy' argument, suggesting that moral sentiments co-ordinate social behaviour among families and similarly close groups, while the price system performs the same task in the impersonal marketplace, an argument with which Hollander (1987) implicitly agrees.

These three arguments for consistency are based on different notions of what 'consistency' means. The first argument claims consistency on the grounds of shared precepts. The second claims consistency in that the theory of TMS gives a necessary condition for the society of WN. The third argument claims that the two theories operate in separable portions of the same world, and that hence they are consistent. This chapter shows that TMS and WN are consistent in another, and perhaps a stronger sense. We prove the existence of general competitive equilibrium in the presence of moral sentiments in the market. We show that assumptions of competition and perfect information are sufficient for this equilibrium to be Pareto-optimal, as they are for an equilibrium without moral sentiments. Furthermore, we show that all but one of the assumptions on moral sentiments which are necessary to achieve the proof of equilibrium have been made by Smith himself.

Moral sentiments and economics

Adam Smith wrote TMS as a work in philosophy and ethics, not as an economic tract. He concerns himself principally with setting up a theory of perception and behaviour based on the assumption of benevolent and imaginative interest in one's fellows. The Impartial Spectator within each man allows him to sympathize imaginatively with the experiences of others, and to see his own actions through the eyes of others. Smith shows how moral sentiments affect human behaviour individually and help co-ordinate society both directly and through the mediation of a system of justice to which the sentiments give rise. Throughout, Smith illustrates his theory not only with examples of day-to-day behaviour, but by the actions and reactions of the famous, thus demonstrating the application of moral sentiments to experience. He concludes by comparing his theory of the formation of ethics to those of other philosophers. We do not claim that Smith was more than marginally concerned with the economics of moral sentiments, or that he set about proving the consistency of moral sentiments and the marketplace. However, Smith noted that

> A free commerce on a fair consideration must appear to be advantageous on both sides. We see that it must be so betwixt individuals, unless one of them be a fool and makes a bargain plainly ruinous; but betwixt prudent men it must always be advantageous (Lectures on Jurisprudence(A)vi. 159–60).

Clearly Smith did not feel that the marketplace was incompatible with increasing the welfare of others. Here, as elsewhere, he mentions the inefficiency caused by imperfect information.

Since moral sentiments affect human choice, they automatically have an economic application. Moreover, several passages in TMS make clear that this application is to demand. Immediately before the Invisible Hand passage of TMS, Smith states that moral sentiments generate a 'deception' which makes men emulate the wealthy and so work for more than their subsistence, thus making economic growth possible. The rich 'are led by an invisible hand to make nearly the same distribution of the necessaries of life which would have been made had the earth been divided into equal portions among all its inhabitants' (TMS, 303–4) since they are unable to consume more 'necessaries' than their bellies can hold, and spend their wealth on the services of others. Hollander (1973) describes this argument, and shrewdly notes Smith's mistaken implication that the wealthy enjoy their servants' enjoyment of income, rather than the wealthy enjoying their own income and the servants theirs. This, surely, is an argument about how moral sentiments influence demand. The poor work to satisfy their demand for more than necessary goods because they would like to occupy the wealthy man's prominent position in the national esteem. Meanwhile, the Invisible Hand of moral sentiments causes the rich to increase others' income through their demand for goods and services. In the *Wealth of Nations*, Smith argues that wages are higher in 'disgraceful' trades (I.x.b.2), and a shortage of labour in such trades is compatible with moral sentiments.

Indeed, Smith implies that moral sentiments help to form the social man's estimate of goods and activities.

> To a man who from his birth was a stranger to society, the objects of his passions, the external bodies which either pleased or hurt him, would occupy his whole attention. ... Bring him into society, and all his own passions will immediately become the causes of new passions. He will observe that mankind approve of some

of them, and are disgusted by others. He will be elevated in one case, and cast down in the other; his desires and aversions, new joys and new sorrows, will now often become the causes of new desires and new sorrows. ... (TMS, 204–205).

By observing the reaction of others to his pleasures, social man learns how he should esteem them. The esteem in which an individual holds the consumption of goods and services orders his preferences over different consumption bundles. Moral sentiments, then, affect the utility function of the individual by affecting his estimate of his pleasures. Moreover, since the individual's moral sentiments cause him to rejoice in the happiness of others, and sympathize with their condition in general, his utility function must include as positive arguments the utilities of those with whom he sympathizes.

Conspicuous consumption, described by Smith as 'the parade of riches, which in [a rich person's] eye is never so complete as when they possess those decisive marks of opulence which nobody can possess but themselves' (WN, I.xi.c.31), is a case of immoral sentiments, where the poor envy the rich and the rich are pleased. Whether an individual's utility is increasing or decreasing in the utilities of others, our argument holds. Equilibrium and Pareto-optimality do not depend on the signs of derivatives of the utility function. Pareto-optimality, however, does not hold without perfect information on others' utility functions.

With perfect information (equivalent to an infallible imagination), which we assume throughout this chapter, the utility function of an individual i with moral sentiments will be of the form

$$u_i = u(x_i, u_j, u_k, \ldots u_z),$$

where u_i is i's utility, x_i the list of goods consumed by i, and for all k, u_k is the utility of individual k, which depends on his consumption and the utility of some set of others. We do not argue that Smith invariably assumes perfect information in TMS, which contains his account of the vain man and the proud man (TMS, 411–20), or in WN, in which he discusses the choice of profession of men too young to have good information (WN, I.x.b.21–9). He is aware of the inefficiency uncertainty causes.

Macfie (1967, p. 59) argues that neither TMS nor WN includes an important part for utility, an opinion which seems to us strongly coloured by the fact that Macfie takes Smith's use of the word 'utility' to be the same as ours and Bentham's. Smith actually uses the word to indicate a sort of gimcrack handiness (see for example, TMS, 297). We have shown, however, that in discussing the opinions of individuals as to the desirability of various consumption bundles, Smith is indeed discussing utility in our sense.

For whom, then, does the individual feel moral sentiments?

After himself, the members of his own family, those who usually live in the same house with him, his parents, his children, his brothers and sisters, are naturally the objects of his warmest affections. ... He knows better how every thing is likely to affect them, and his sympathy with them is more precise and determinate, than it can be with the greater part of other people. ... Among well-disposed people, the necessity or conveniency of mutual accommodation, very frequently produces a friendship not unlike that which takes place among those who are born to live in the same family. ... Even the trifling circumstances of living in the same neighbourhood, has some effect of the same kind. ... (TMS, 359–66).

Although Smith specifically suggests that even an individual with moral sentiments will not care greatly about the happiness of an unknown Chinese, the web of moral sentiments may none the less spread quite far. In a neo-classical model, we cannot be sure who the j through z individuals whose welfare i cares about are. If all individuals in an economy care only about the welfare of individuals with whom they have no commercial transactions, then the inclusion of others' utility in i's utility function does not affect equilibrium. In this case, the 'spheres of intimacy' argument holds without need for further elaboration. But Smith gives us no grounds to suppose that moral sentiments are so limited. If the butcher, the brewer, or the baker live in the individual's neighbourhood, he is liable to feel sympathy with them. A more general argument than that of 'spheres of intimacy', then, is required to show that moral sentiments and the invisible hand of the price system can coexist in the same economy.

Toynbee (1884, p. 137) claims that classical economics, 'an insult to the simple natural piety of human affections', lost 'the bitter argument between economists and human beings' when the labour question was addressed. He holds that Smith regarded self-interest as excluding altruism, and that the existence of altruism refutes Smith. Polanyi (1944) feels that the classical notion that markets should prevail disrupted nineteenth century society, since men are not income-maximizing but social creatures. Clearly, so long as moral sentiments are compatible with the market theory of the *Wealth of Nations*, these views do not hold for the economics of Smith. Furthermore, Hollander (1985) shows that for Bentham, another classical economist, moral sentiments must be added to utilitarianism for a just society to exist (Hollander (1985, pp. 616–17), Bentham (1789)).

Lastly, do moral sentiments affect the supply side of the economy? We use supply here in the competitive general equilibrium sense of the supply of produced goods and services. We would expect moral sentiments to affect the supply of labour, but this is not a produced good. In terms of a competitive model, labour is treated as a part of each individual's endowment, which he may trade for other goods or consume directly, and labour thus enters the consumer's problem through his budget constraint. Smith believed that moral sentiments would indeed affect labour supply by causing individuals, through their emulation of wealth, to work longer than would be necessary for subsistence (TMS, 303).

There is no passage in TMS suggesting that Smith thought moral sentiments affect the supply decisions of firms. Similarly, though less interestingly, there is little suggestion in WN that anything but profit-maximization subject to uncertainty enters into supply behaviour. As Smith states, 'I have never known much good done by those who affected to trade for the publick good. It is an affectation, indeed, not very common among merchants, and very few words need be employed in dissuading them from it' (WN, IV. ii.9). (There is little in WN about the determinants of demand. While the economic application of TMS is to demand, WN is largely about supply.) It is not clear that moral sentiments need influence supply behaviour at all: certainly the usual assumption of strictly personal utility maximization is not inconsistent with profit maximization in competitive firms. Diamond and Mirrlees (1973) do not suggest that production decisions are affected by a consumption externality.

It is not argued here, or below, that moral sentiments in utility fail to influence the set of equilibrium price vectors. Indeed, one would expect the price of labour to be affected. In this sense moral sentiments can indirectly influence supply behaviour, though not the way in which supply decisions are made. It might seem reasonable to suppose that moral sentiments could influence the behaviour of monopsonists in hiring labour, or of monopolists in selling final products. Collard (1978) cites J. K. Whitaker's account of Marshall's notion that a perfectly altruistic monopolist will behave like a competitor, due to an equal weighting of producer and consumer surplus. Smith, who wrote that 'People of the same trade seldom meet together, even for merriment and diversion, but the conversation ends in a conspiracy against the publick, or in some contrivance to raise prices' (WN, I.x.c.27), is certainly aware of the existence of monopoly. Furthermore, he was aware of the inefficiencies monopoly induces:

> By perpetual monopoly, all other subjects of the state are taxed very absurdly in two different ways; first, by the high price of goods, which, in the case of a free trade, they could buy much cheaper; and, secondly, by their total exclusion from a branch of business, which it might be both convenient and profitable for many of them to carry on [WN, V.i.e.30].

Here, however, we follow the usual track in assuming firms are competitive in both input and output markets, taking prices as data.

Smith notes in WN that 'Sometimes, indeed, the liberality of the landlord, makes him accept of somewhat less than this portion' which is 'the highest the tenant can afford to pay in the actual circumstances of the land' (WN, I.xi.a.1). Where a landlord behaves this way because of liking for his tenant, however, this action may be treated as a transfer of the landlord's endowment, and not as a market transaction. This leaves us able still to assume competitive markets and remain true to Smith.

We therefore assume that moral sentiments affect the demand functions for goods and labour supply through interdependent utility, while supply is determined on the usual cost minimizing, profit maximizing basis.

Proof of equilibrium

It has not been generally recognized that equilibrium can exist where moral sentiments enter utility functions without a specific functional form being assumed. Wilson (1976) states without argument that non-tuism, or disinterest in the welfare of the person one is trading with, is necessary for the market to 'work' in the same sense that it is necessary for a game of chess to 'work'. Others, however, have examined the nature of equilibrium or its Pareto-properties when non-tuism does not hold; for example, Whitaker's account of Marshall's altruistic monopolist who generates the normal competitive equilibrium. Edgeworth discusses a case in which B's utility enters additively into A's utility function and vice versa (Edgeworth (1881), 53, n.l; cf. Collard (1978)), a case of linear moral sentiments. Similarly, Diamond and Mirrlees (1973) examine the case in which A feels a utility–externality from B's consumption of a particular good and vice versa, with utility from all other consumption entering additively, proxied by income which is not spent on the externality-generating good. This is the case of separable moral sentiments (if the externality is positive) in one good only.

We make no assumption as to the separability or linearity of moral sentiments in the individual's utility function. As mentioned above, we assume perfect information on the utilities of others, which does not affect the existence of equilibrium but does give Pareto-properties that do not hold with uncertainty. Since we have assumed that moral sentiments do not affect the supply functions of firms, assumptions underlying these are conventional and undiscussed here.

Below, we give the assumptions necessary for the usual Brouwer's fixed point proof of equilibrium to hold. For this, we need a continuous excess demand function

$$\left[\sum_i \sum_j (D_{ia}(p) - S_{ja}(p) - w_{ia}) = z_a(p) \right]$$

to exist for each good a, where i indexes consumers and j firms, and w_{ia} represents i's endowment of good a. Since we assume conventional supply functions for each firm, aggregate supply is continuous and upward sloping. In order to be able to use Brouwer's fixed point theorem to prove equilibrium, we need first to achieve continuous aggregate demand for each good in the presence of moral sentiments. Brouwer's fixed point theorem states that any continuous mapping from the price space onto itself has a fixed point at which the mapping of a price vector is that price vector. Using continuous excess demand functions we can construct a continuous mapping whose fixed point is by definition equilibrium. By Brouwer's theorem, that point exists and therefore so does equilibrium. We make the usual assumptions about non-satiation, continuity of the utility function in all arguments, and the timelessness (or one period nature) of the economy. We do not argue that Smith made these assumptions.

Convergent echo effects

Since i's utility is a function of his own consumption and the utilities of individuals j through z, it is possible that the utility of these individuals may not be finite, even for a given distribution of goods. Suppose that A receives a finite amount of satisfaction directly from her consumption bundle, and that she and B have moral sentiments toward each other. B's utility is then augmented by A's satisfaction. But B's increased utility increases A's, and so forth. It is conceivable that feedback through the interlinked utility functions of individuals could prevent finite utilities from occurring.

According to Smith, however, 'the emotion of the spectator will still be very apt to fall short of the violence of what is felt by [the principal]' (TMS, 66). This argues that the addition to B's utility from A's direct satisfaction will be less than A's direct-satisfaction, that A's reaction to B's reaction will be smaller than B's reaction, and so forth. Smith has given the necessary condition for convergence of utility despite the echo effects of moral sentiments. A's utility is convex in B's, and vice versa, so that A's (B's) utility increases by decreasing increments. This is necessary but not sufficient for both utilities to converge, as we can see by recalling that the series

$$\sum_{k=1}^{n} (1/k)$$

does not converge as $n \to \infty$.

Smith introduces the 'desire for concord', a mechanism derived from moral sentiments, which gives the sufficient condition for convergence.

> The person principally concerned is sensible of [his spectator's incomplete participation], and at the same time passionately desires a more complete sympathy. He longs for that relief which nothing can afford him but the entire concord of the affections of the spectators with his own. ....[He] can only hope to obtain this by lowering his passion to that pitch, in which the spectators are capable of going along with him. ... In order to produce this concord, as nature teaches the spectators to assume the circumstances of the person principally concerned, so she teaches this last in some measure to assume those of the spectators. As they are continually placing themselves in his situation, and thence conceiving emotions similar to what he feels; so he is constantly placing himself in theirs, and thence conceiving some degree of that coolness about his own fortune, with which he is sensible that they will view it. ... We are immediately put in mind of the light in which [a spectator]

will view our situation, and we begin ourselves to view it in the same light; for the effect of sympathy is instantaneous (TMS, 67–8).

Because the spectator's sympathy with the consumer is less intense than his feelings about his own activities, and because the consumer wants to achieve a 'concord' of sympathy with his spectator, the consumer's direct satisfaction is moderated until such concord is achieved, and consumer and spectator reach finite utility instantaneously. We can write this: for all x_i, x_j, ..., x_z, and i, $u_i(x_i, u_j, ..., u_z) = a \in R$. This allows us to write $u_i(x_i, u_j, ..., u_z) = f^i(x_i, x_j, ..., x_z)$. It should be noted that the j through z individuals of $u(\cdot)$ are a subset of the j through z individuals of $f(\cdot)$. The arguments of $u(\cdot)$ are the utilities of those i cares about, but the arguments of $f(\cdot)$ are the consumption bundles of those i cares about plus anyone else they care about.

No matter what the distribution of goods, each individual has a finite utility even when his utility depends on that of others. West (1976) refers to this as Smith's 'emotional equilibrium', and it is indeed an equilibrium in the sense of a guarantee of convergence.

Continuity
We assume that for all x_i in a neighbourhood N around x^*_i, $f^i(x_i, x_j, ..., x_z)$ is in a neighbourhood M around a, where $a = f^i(x^*_i, x_j, ..., x_z)$. This is simply an assumption that each utility function is continuous in the consumer's consumption. Each morally sentimental utility function $f^i(\cdot)$ is continuously differentiable. We would like to assume as well that $f^i(\cdot)$ is twice continuously differentiable for each consumer i.

Although his library included three works on 'fluxions', that is to say, calculus (Yanaihara (1966), p. 84), Smith made no continuity assumption in TMS. Yet this is the very assumption one would not expect him to make: almost the only form of mathematics used in economics in the eighteenth century was political arithmetic, of which Smith was sceptical. Schumpeter (1954, p. 466) states that von Thünen, who first published in 1826, was 'first to use the calculus as a form of economic reasoning'. It seems unlikely, therefore, that Smith would assume the purely mathematical property of continuity in a philosophical work on moral sentiments.

We assume the continuity of each individual's utility function so that we can write it as a differentiable function of a set of consumption bundles. This is necessary for us to derive each individual's demand function. We assume the utility function is twice continuously differentiable in order to ensure that each individual's demand function is continuous.

Derivation of the individual's demand function
Each consumer i now faces the problem,

$$\max f^i (x_i, x_j, \ldots, x_z) \text{ subject to}$$

$$p \cdot x_i \le p \cdot (w_i + t_i \cdot \sum_j y_j),$$

where t_i is the vector of i's shares in each firm in the economy, and y_j is the netput vector of firm j. The left-hand side of the inequality is the cost of i's consumption bundle, which must not exceed the right-hand side, his budget. The first order conditions of the solution of this problem are, for all goods a,

$$f^i_a(\cdot) - p_a \le 0, \text{ where any a will be consumed, and}$$

$$p \cdot x_i - p \cdot (w_i + t_i \cdot \sum_j y_j) \le 0, \text{ due to non-satiation.}$$

These first order conditions give a continuous demand function for each individual, for each good. It should be noted, moreover, that morally sympathetic marginal utility takes into account the increased satisfaction of a sympathetic society when i consumes one more unit of a. The result is similar to that depicted by Hogarth in the prints *Beer Street* and *Gin Lane*. Where the respectable beer is consumed, all society is healthy and productive, but consumption of wicked gin leads to universal depravity. Goods considered reputable will be consumed more, and those considered reprehensible less, with moral sentiments, because a positive (negative) marginal utility will be more positive (negative). This is consistent with Smith's account of vanity and pride (TMS, 411–20), since both proud and vain people are said to concern themselves with others's esteem of their economic position. The vain man differs from the proud one in that he is willing to fool his spectators about where his budget constraint lies and appear richer than he is.

Since we have assumed perfect information, we have assumed vain men away. We have also assumed that the utility-externality is completely internalized, since the consumer with perfect information takes social repercussions fully into account in formulating his demand. It is this that makes the morally sentimental equilibrium with perfect information Pareto-optimal.

We cannot be sure that these demand functions are downward sloping. This is, of course, true of demand functions where moral sentiments do not enter into the utility function. In that case, a good may be so inferior that income effects outweigh substitution effects, and the demand curve slopes upward. Where moral sentiments enter into i's utility function, suppose that his direct reaction to good a is such that it is inferior. If this view is held by all of those whose utilities he cares about, and who care about his utility, then a is a more inferior good than it would be if moral sentiments did not exist. Since moral sentiments can strengthen the inferiority of a good, it follows that Giffen goods are more likely when there are moral sentiments than when there are not.

Since each consumer consumes within his budget set, all demands are feasible. There exists a finite price for each good at which demand is less than or equal to supply plus endowment.

Proofs of the existence and Pareto-optimality of equilibrium sketched
With the assumptions given above, we have derived market demand functions continuous in price for all goods. With the usual continuous supply functions, we have continuous excess demand functions. With a mapping from the price space onto itself which uses the excess demand functions and is thus continuous, we can use Brouwer's fixed point theorem to show that an equilibrium price vector exists. With perfect information and competition, Pareto-optimality follows by the proof given in Arrow and Hahn (1971).

Conclusion

We have shown that, so far as Adam Smith's *Theory of Moral Sentiments* pertains to economics, it affects the demand side through the utility function. We have given the extra conditions on a utility function with moral sentiments which are necessary for the proof of the existence of competitive equilibrium, and shown that only the assumption of continuity has not been given by Smith. Lastly, we showed that this equilibrium allocation is efficient in the sense of being Pareto-optimal. This completes our proof from Smith's text that moral sentiments are consistent with the invisible hand of the price system.

Note

1. We are grateful to Samuel Hollander, Rik Kleer, and the participants in Professor Hollander's workshop in history of economic thought at the University of Toronto for helpful comments.

References

Anspach, R. (1972), 'The Implications of the *Theory of Moral Sentiments* for Adam Smith's Economic Thought', *History of Political Economy*, 4, 176–206.

Arrow, K.J. and Hahn, F.H. (1971), *General Competitive Equilibrium*, Amsterdam: North-Holland.

Bentham, J. (1789), *An Introduction to the Principles of Morals and Legislation*, eds. J.H. Burns and H.L.A. Hart, London.

Campbell, W.F. (1967), 'Adam Smith's Theory of Justice, Prudence, and Beneficence', *American Economic Review*, 57, 571–7.

Collard, D. (1978), *Economics and Altruism*, New York: Oxford University Press.

Danner, P.L. (1976), 'Sympathy and Exchangeable Value: Keys to Adam Smith's Social Philosophy', *Review of Social Economy*, 34, 317–31.

Diamond, P.A. and Mirrlees, J.A. (1973), 'Aggregate Production with Consumption Externalities', *Quarterly Journal of Economics*, 1–24.

Edgeworth, F.Y. (1881), *Mathematical Psychics*, London: Kegan Paul.

Hollander, S. (1973), *The Economics of Adam Smith*, Toronto: University of Toronto Press.

Hollander, S. (1985), *The Economics of John Stuart Mill*, Toronto: University of Toronto Press.
Hollander, S. (1987), *Classical Economics*, Oxford: Basil Blackwell.
Macfie, A.L. (1967). *The Individual in Society: Papers on Adam Smith*, London: George Allen & Unwin.
Nieli, R. (1986), 'Spheres of Intimacy and the Adam Smith Problem', *Journal of the History of Ideas*, 611–24 .
Oncken, A. (1897), 'The Consistency of Adam Smith', *Economic Journal* 7, 443–50.
Polanyi, K. (1944), *The Great Transformation*, New York: Farrar & Rinehart.
Schumpeter, J.A. (1954), *History of Economic Analysis*, ed. E.B. Schumpeter, New York: Oxford University Press.
Smith, A. (1759), *The Theory of Moral Sentiments*, reprinted (1976) with an introduction by E.G. West, Indianapolis: Liberty Press.
Smith, A. (1776), *An Inquiry into the Nature and Causes of the Wealth of Nations*, reprinted (1981), eds R.H. Campbell, A.S. Skinner, and W.B. Todd, Indianapolis: Liberty Classics.
Smith, A. (1982), *Lectures on Jurisprudence*, eds R.L. Meek, D.D. Raphael, and P.G. Stein, Indianapolis: Liberty Classics.
Teichgraeber, R.F. (1986), *'Free Trade' and Moral Philosophy: Rethinking the Sources of Adam Smith's Wealth of Nations,* Durham, N.C.: Duke University Press.
Toynbee, A. (1884), *Lectures on the Industrial Revolution in England*, ed. W.J. Ashley, London: Longmans Green.
Viner, J. (1968), 'Adam Smith', *International Encyclopedia of the Social Sciences*, vol. 14, 322–9, New York: Macmillan and the Free Press.
West, E.G. (1976), 'Introduction', *The Theory of Moral Sentiments*, Indianapolis: Liberty Press.
Wilson, T. (1976), 'Sympathy and Self-Interest', *The Market and the State: Essays in Honour of Adam Smith*, eds T. Wilson and A.S. Skinner, Oxford: The Clarendon Press.
Yanaihara, T. (1966), *Catalogue of Adam Smith's Library*, New York: Augustus M. Kelley.

6 The 'rigid' wages fund doctrine: McCulloch, Mill and the 'monster' of money

John Vint

Introduction

J.R. McCulloch has been seen by some historians of economic thought as having an important historical role in the development of the wages fund doctrine. For Schumpeter (1954, p. 669) he was the 'leading exponent' of the doctrine. O'Brien (1970, p. 360, n4) quotes Bonar (1885, p. 272) as arguing that McCulloch was the author of the doctrine. In fact, however, Bonar put the case as follows:

> The theory of the wages fund was formed from the facts of a perfectly exceptional time, and on the strengths of two truths misapplied, the doctrine of Malthus (on Population) in its most unripe form, and of Ricardo (on Value) in its most abstract. J.R. McCulloch seems to have been the first who put the two together to deduce a rigid law of wages (1885, p. 272).

Thus it is rigidity that Bonar is referring to and not authorship. He refers to Mrs. Marcet as having put the case 'more carefully' in 1817 (1885, p. 272), and he was not the only one to link Marcet and McCulloch together. Thus Cannan argued:

> That the rate of wages depends on the proportion between the labouring population and 'capital' had been laid down in Mrs. Marcet's *Conversations*. But it was reserved for McCulloch to give definiteness and rigidity to Mrs. Marcet's doctrine by illustrating it with an arithmetical example (1893, p. 263)[1].

In addition to Jane Marcet's contribution in the *Conversations*, other elements of the doctrine were apparent in the work of Smith, Malthus and Ricardo. We shall return to the arithmetical example shortly, but it is clear from what has been said that McCulloch has been seen by well-known historians of economic thought to be a prominent exponent of a 'rigid' wages fund analysis which *may* have originated with Marcet's *Conversations*.

In contrast to McCulloch, J. S. Mill is commonly associated with the *demise* of the wages fund doctrine. The reasons for, and the nature of his recantation in 1869 have been the subject of a number of interpretations,[2] and the issue is likely to remain of interest to historians as one of the few examples where a major piece of theory was explicitly denied by one of its erstwhile leading proponents.

This paper focuses on the respective roles of McCulloch and Mill in the development and decline of the wages fund doctrine. We shall argue that McCulloch can indeed be regarded as the author of a 'rigid' version of the wages fund doctrine but for reasons different from those given by Bonar and Cannan. The rigidity developed by McCulloch was to protect the idea of a predetermined real wages fund from the notion of wages paid in money. We shall argue that the assumption required to ensure this rigidity was not subscribed to consistently by other Classical writers such as Ricardo and J.S. Mill himself. Indeed we shall argue that it was the continuing dichotomy between real and money conceptions of the analysis that paved the way finally for Mill's recantation in 1869.

Our analysis is undertaken using a Lakatosian framework modified in a number of ways. Such a framework is most useful for looking at an issue such as the wages fund doctrine since it contains tools and concepts designed to deal with questions relating to the progress and decline of theories.[3] We will argue along with Fisher (1986) that in applying Lakatos's ideas, appropriate account must be taken of his earlier work *Proofs and Refutations* (1976) as well as the more familiar article 'Falsification and the Methodology of Scientific Research Programmes' (1970) and that this earlier work proves particularly useful in highlighting McCulloch's role.

A Lakatosian framework
The basic features of Lakatos's approach – the methodology of scientific research programmes – are now quite widely known and we shall not spend time rehearsing them. Our approach will rest firmly on the Lakatosian model but with a number of qualifications and it is to two of these that we now turn.

Many Lakatosian studies undertaken by economists have focused on the discipline as a whole and have postulated a hard core built usually from economic man or perfect competition assumptions (see, for example, Latsis (1976), Blaug (1976) and O'Brien (1976)). Often these studies have gone on to discuss the changes from Classical to NeoClassical, or NeoClassical to Keynesian economics. Fulton (1984) has argued that these hard core formulations differ in character from the sort of hard core that Lakatos had in mind and which was to consist of specific laws or axioms.[4] Thus, if applied properly, the Lakatosian analysis in economics could be used to identify a research programme at the sub-discipline level, the hard core of which would consist of a set of formal theoretical statements. The economic man and competitive assumptions would then be given the status of 'presuppositions'.[5] Fulton then applies this approach to the theory of the firm and refers to two other studies which have used this smaller scale with success (see de Marchi (1976) and Blaug (1980)).

This approach is clearly very useful in enabling us to examine the development of a *specific* doctrine such as the wages fund theory. Such a Lakatosian hard core for a Classical wages theory research programme may have the following elements:

1. Wages are advances of real wage goods made from capital by capitalists to workers.
2. A predetermined fund of wage goods is set aside by the capitalists at the beginning of the production period.
3. The supply of labour in the short run is fixed.
4. The real wage rate in the short run is determined by dividing the predetermined wage fund by the labour supply.
5. In the long run increases or decreases in capital accumulation will lead to increases or decreases in the wages fund.
6. In the long run the population may change in response to changes in the real wage rate.
7. The trend of the wage rate over time will depend on the relationship between capital accumulation and population growth, assuming constant technology.

We thus have a hard core which consists of two parts. One, the short run wages theory – the wage fund doctrine – is composed of statements 1–4, and the second, the long run theory, is composed of statements 5–7. What we have here in effect are two 'laws' – the wages fund doctrine, on the one hand, and the population principle, on the other. This set of hard core statements performs two functions. First, it contains the key elements of the typical view of Classical wage theory as portrayed in twentieth century literature. Second, in a full study it would enable us to undertake an assessment of the extent to which an actual hard core and associated research programme emerged resembling this hypothetical Lakatosian stereotype and to trace its subsequent history.[6] In this paper we shall limit ourselves to a discussion of only one aspect of this, namely the impact on the wages fund doctrine of a major potential counter-example.

Another typical feature of the economic applications of Lakatos has been the lack of attention paid to his earlier work in *Proofs and Refutations* (1976) as Fisher (1986) has recently pointed out. The initial contribution in *Proofs and Refutations* focused on the ways in which a mathematical conjecture (prediction) could be defended against counter-examples or modified to take account of them. This work formed a very important foundation stone of Lakatos's whole approach because it discussed ways in which a mathematician may resist or postpone the consequences of counter-evidence. It is this resistance or postponement which distinguishes the 'sophisticated' falsificationism of Lakatos from the 'dogmatic' falsificationism of Popper in which counter-examples result in the immediate abandonment of theories. In this early work Lakatos was dealing with questions concerning mathematical discovery but it is clear that the arguments presented are relevant to and underpin the later work on the Methodology of Scientific Research Programmes (hereafter MSRP) which is meant to be a model applicable to all science. There are few references to the earlier work in the MSRP article, but Lakatos does make it clear in one footnote that it can be seen as a 'detailed case study' of the arguments being put forward concerning research programmes, although the notion of a research programme had not been developed at the time of writing *Proofs and Refutations* (1976, p. 135).

The result of the lack of attention to the early work, Fisher argues, is that much of the debate has focused on the subsequent and later questions of what constitutes the hard core, the protective belt and so on. What this has meant in general terms is that little effort has been spent in examining in detail the strategies of defence and consolidation which economists, like other scientists, have employed.

In *Proofs and Refutations*, Lakatos classifies responses to counter-examples according to whether they result in a decrease or increase in content. Altogether five content-decreasing responses are identified – *(a)* surrender, *(b)* monster-barring, *(c)* monster-adjustment, *(d)* exception-barring, *(e)* lemma-incorporation. According to Lakatos, surrender takes place if in the face of a global counter-example a theory or model is abandoned. The example that Fisher gives of this in economics is that of the 'discovery' of the upward sloping demand curve as a global counter-example to Walrasian economics which predicts that all demand curves are downward sloping. Surrender here would mean the abandonment of all Walrasian economics and would be a good example of 'dogmatic falsificationism' at work in economics. It is a central thrust of Lakatos's work that this in fact does not typically happen in the development of science. There is much to be lost in throwing out the *whole* Walrasian project and scientists are reluctant to abandon theories in the absence of any alternatives. Fisher refers to the wages fund issue in this context, arguing that attacks on the doctrine did not result in the 'failure' of Classical economics which only came about as a result of the rise of marginalism (1986, p. 14). However, it is not quite clear what is meant by 'failure' here. Fisher is presumably *not* talking about abandonment, for important parts of Classical theory survived into the twentieth century to confront Keynes, and if he is not talking about abandonment it is hard to see the relevance of this to the question of surrender. The problem that Fisher is running up against here and avoiding is the issue of the level at which Lakatos's approach is most appropriately applied. As we have argued above, the most appropriate level is that of particular doctrines and in those terms the question of the abandonment of Classical wage theory (as opposed to *all* Classical economics) is problematic.

'Monster-barring' refers to the process by which definitions are respecified so that the 'monster' – the counter-example – is barred on the grounds that it does not meet the specification of the model. The example that Fisher provides of this in the work of Jevons is where he defines a market as perfectly competitive which, since his theory is only meant to apply to markets, 'bars' the monster of monopoly (1986, pp. 176–8). The scientist who employs the technique of 'monster-adjusment' reinterprets the counter-example as consistent with the theory. Thus in Jevons's work, substitute commodities are potential counter-examples to the equations of exchange. Jevons deals with this by reinterpreting substitutes as one homogeneous commodity of variable strength which brings them within the scope of the theory.

With the strategies of 'exception-barring' and 'lemma-incorporation', more effort is made to take the counter-example seriously than with the previous two techniques. The exception-barrer will provide a list of exceptions to the theory as Jevons did with his 'Failures of the Equations of Exchange' where cases of indivisibility were pointed out as anomalous. The problem with this is that the demonstration or proof of the old theory no longer applies to the new. This problem is overcome in the technique of 'lemma-incorporation'. Here, when faced with a global counter-example, the scientist searches for the lemma which will provide the *local* counter-example. Thus, with the Giffen goods case referred to earlier, the addition of another lemma that the utility functions are additive gives the theorem 'the demand curves of individuals with additive utility functions are downward sloping'. Now the old proof still works for the new theorem. The new theorem is more limited of course – there has been some loss in content but this has been kept to a minimum compared with the result that may have been obtained by exception-barring, which may have led to the theorem 'the demand curves for normal goods are downward sloping' (1986, p. 16). This latter proposition is of course more limited in that the demand curves for most inferior goods are downward sloping.

All of these strategies then suffer from weaknesses. The method of surrender leads to total abandonment of a theory which could possibly be saved by further theoretical adjustment. Monster-barring and monster-adjustment inhibit the growth of theories because the criticism offered by the counter-example is muted and hidden either in a change of definitions or empirical reinterpretation. Exception-barring has some merit in that the implications of the counter-example are not avoided but at the same time the proof is weakened. Lemma-incorporation is the 'least worst' of these strategies in that the proof is retained albeit with some reduction in content. Thus not all the predictive power of the old theory survives the addition of the lemma.

None of these strategies is as satisfactory as those which increase the content of a theory by adjusting the theoretical arguments in such a way that the counter-example is turned into a corroboration of the theory. Such content-increasing responses may be undertaken by replacing the lemma that provided the local counter-example, adding auxiliary hypotheses or making semantic changes such as concept-stretching where the meaning of terms is expanded. The example that Fisher gives of this refers back again to the Giffen case (1986, p. 17). We saw when dealing with lemma-incorporation that the addition of the assumption of an additive utility function deals with the counter-example (the upward sloping demand curve) by limiting the new theory to apply to only those individuals with additive utility functions. If this lemma is now replaced by a general utility function, the theory predicts both downward and upward sloping demand curves under certain conditions. The new theory then explains the counter-example while retaining the former unrefuted content. This early work of Lakatos in *Proofs* is very important, for it underpins his later contributions and will provide us with some useful concepts with which to approach the ways in which Classical wage theory was rendered immune from attacks.

Before going on to discuss McCulloch's work, it will be useful to review the extent to which a Lakatosian hard core appeared in the work of some major Classical writers who preceded him. This work has been undertaken more fully in an earlier paper,[7] and it is only possible to present the briefest discussion here. An examination of the work of Smith, Malthus and Ricardo reveals that some elements of the hard core as we have specified it are present in these early studies. The long run hard core is well established and it is usually accompanied by the additional hypothesis that population will grow faster than capital. The short run hard core is less well developed. The notion that wages are paid from capital is present but there is no evidence of any explicit statement that funds for the maintenance of workers are predetermined in any way. Although it is implicit in many of the early statements that the wage rate is determined by the relationship of capital to population, even this fundamental point is nowhere stated as clearly and simply as in the work of Jane Marcet referred to above, although her unqualified use of the term capital is not without its own difficulties. Also present in these early works was a question that was to bedevil the wages fund doctrine throughout its history and that was the question of whether the fund should be seen in real or money terms.

J.R. McCulloch and the 'monster' of money

McCulloch's views on wages are contained in two main works, *The Principles of Political Economy* (1825) and the *Essay on Wages* (1826), revised and enlarged as the *Treatise on the Rate of Wages* (1854). In the chapter on wages in *The Principles* he outlines the elements of a wages fund approach:

> The capacity of a country to support and employ labourers is not directly dependent on the advantageousness of situation, richness of soil, or extent of territory. These, undoubtedly, are circumstances of very great importance, and must have a powerful influence in determining the rate at which a people *advances* in the career of wealth

and civilization. But it is obviously not on these circumstances, *but on the actual amount of the accumulated produce of previous labour, or of capital, devoted to the payment of wages, in the possession of a country, at any given period*, that its power of supporting and employing labourers must wholly depend. A fertile soil affords the means of rapidly increasing capital; but that is all. Before this soil can be cultivated, capital must be provided for the support of the labourers employed upon it, just as it must be provided for the support of those engaged in manufactures, or in any other department of industry (1825, p. 173).[8]

This is a very clear statement – arguably the first by a major Classical economist – of the predetermined nature of the wages fund. Mrs. Marcet may have been the first to argue that wages depended on the 'proportion which capital bears to the labouring population', but in her work the predetermined nature of the wages fund can only be inferred from her discussion of the example of a 'shipwreck' where a new supply of labour is brought to a desert island dragging down the wage rate as the newcomers compete for employment. By contrast McCulloch, in the passage quoted above, argues explicitly that a country's ability to employ workers depends on the existence of an 'amount of the accumulated produce of previous labour'.[9] McCulloch goes on to explain the determination of the wage rate:

> It is a necessary consequence of this principle, that the amount of subsistence falling to each labourer, or the *rate* of wages, must depend on the proportion which the whole capital bears to the whole amount of the labouring population. If the amount of capital were increased, without a corresponding increase taking place in the population, a larger share of such capital would fall to each individual, or the rate of wages would be augmented: And if, on the other hand, population were increased faster than capital, a less share would be apportioned to each individual, or the rate of wages would be reduced (1825, p. 173).

Having been very careful to spell out, in the first quoted passage, that the ability of a country to support workers depends on the amount of previously accumulated capital 'devoted to the payment of wages', McCulloch now writes more loosely of the 'proportion which the whole capital bears to the whole amount of the labouring population'. However, the numerical example referred to by Cannan, and now at this point developed by McCulloch to illustrate his argument, clearly shows that it is only that part of capital devoted to wages that is involved in wage rate determination:

> To illustrate this principle, let us suppose, that the capital of a country appropriated to the payment of wages, would, if reduced to the standard of wheat, form a mass of 10,000,000, of quarters: If the number of labourers in that country were *two* millions, it is evident that the wages of each, reducing them all to the same common standard, would be five quarters: and it is further evident, that this rate of wages could not be increased otherwise, than by increasing the quantity of capital in a

greater proportion than the number of labourers, or by diminishing the number of labourers in a greater proportion than the quantity of capital (1825, p. 173).

In this numerical example then McCulloch argues that the wage rate is found simply by dividing a wages fund by the number of workers.

So far the discussion has been in *real* terms, concerned with the quantity of wages 'rated in commodities'. We are of course not to deduce that McCulloch thought that wages were actually *paid* in wheat – the example was purely illustrative. A few pages later McCulloch emphasizes that labourers' wages are usually paid in money and he counters very firmly the objection that wages will depend more on the amount of *money* in circulation than on the amount of capital:

> The wages of labour are most commonly either paid or estimated in money; and it may perhaps be thought, that their amount will, in consequence, depend more on the quantity of money in circulation in a country, than on the magnitude of its capital. It is really, however, quite the same to the labourer whether the quantity of money received by him as wages is great or small. He will always receive such a quantity as will suffice to put him in possession of a portion of the national capital falling to his share. Men cannot subsist on coin or paper. Where wages are paid in money, the labourers must exchange it for necessaries and conveniences; and it is not the quantity of money they receive but the quantity of necessaries and conveniences for which money will exchange, that is to be considered as really forming their wages. If the quantity of money in Great Britain were reduced by a half, the rate of wages, estimated in money, would decline in the same proportion; but unless some change had, at the same time, taken place in the amount of that portion of the capital of the country which consists of food, clothes and other articles consumed by the labourer, he would continue in precisely the same position. He would carry a smaller quantity of pieces of gold and silver to market than formerly; but he would obtain the same quantity of commodities in exchange for them (1825, p. 174).

This is a very important contribution. As we argued above, from the outset the wages fund discussion was bedevilled by the question of whether it was a *money* or a *real* fund, and this continued to be a source of confusion and debate. McCulloch attempted to argue that money made no difference to the underlying idea that workers would only be able to obtain what had been set aside for them to obtain. Workers, it is argued, spend their money wages on a fixed quantity of workers' wage goods consisting of food, clothing and other articles consumed by the labourer. Any change in money wages will not alter the real wage of the worker or the portion of the national capital falling to his share. If money allocations to labour fall or rise, prices will adjust so that labourers can still just purchase the quantity of wage goods set aside. It is clearly implicit in this argument that workers only consume from that portion of the country's capital which is available in the form of wage goods, and will not consume luxury goods or labour services consumed by capitalists. Without this implicit assumption, the conclusions which McCulloch draws could not be arrived at. His approach here can usefully be analysed using the concepts developed by Lakatos in *Proofs and Refutations*.

For Lakatos, potential counter-examples were 'monsters' and for McCulloch the monster was money. The notion that wages were paid in money was potentially extremely damaging to the idea of a predetermined wages fund and an indication that McCulloch was keen to develop such an idea is provided in his reference in the quotation above to the irrelevance from the worker's point of view of the size of his money wage, for whatever the sum it will only enable him to obtain that produce 'falling to his share'. Faced with the monster and not wishing to surrender, McCulloch was faced with very little real choice of what strategy to adopt. Given the importance of money and the fact that most wages were paid in money, he could hardly engage in monster-barring and argue that the monster does not meet the specification of the model. To do this would be to limit the wages fund argument to the agricultural sector and to those parts of it where workers were still directly maintained by produce stored up from the previous harvest. It is also hard to see how monster-adjustment could take place. This would require some special interpretation of money to bring it into line with the theory and it is difficult to imagine what this could be. It is not possible simply to assume that money has the same characteristics or that it behaves in the same way as wage goods without making some further assumptions and to make further assumptions is to adjust the model and not the monster. Again, exception-barring is not really an option where the exception to be barred is money wages.

The option that is left and the one that McCulloch implicitly adopted was lemma incorporation. The addition of the new lemma improves the theorem although it results in some limited loss of content. The lemma that McCulloch was implicitly incorporating was the assumption that workers only consume wage goods and never consume luxuries. Given this and a predetermined quantity of wage goods, an increase in money wages will only increase goods prices proportionally to leave the workers no better off. Thus, regardless of what is happening to money wages, the real wage fund remains constant. Thus we now have the improved but more limited theorem that 'the average wage rate of workers who are assumed to consume no luxuries is determined by dividing the predetermined wage fund by the labouring population'. The payment of wages in money is not a counter-example to this more restricted but logically stronger and more rigid theorem. It seems likely that it was this version of the wages fund doctrine which underlay much of the later discussion concerning the futility of union activity to raise wages.[10] With this truly rigid version of the doctrine the fundamental question of whether the wages fund was in real or money terms is dealt with completely. While there may be other problems with the analysis, this weakness with the hard core is eradicated.

Had the majority of Classical writers clearly subscribed to and stood by this version, we would be able to say that the hard core had hardened, a process which is allowed for by Lakatos, into a more limited but more consistent form. However, the majority of Classical writers did not consistently outline this version and some argued explicitly against it. Ricardo, for example, had already considered the effect of increasing money allocations to labour. In the chapter in the *Principles* on 'Taxes on Raw Produce', he argued that the worker may not spend all of the increase on food but will spend some of it on 'the other enjoyments of the labourer' (Ricardo (1817), pp. 162–3) and a similar view is outlined in his chapter dealing with Malthus's views on rent (see Ricardo, (1817), pp. 406–7). Again, in correspondence with Trower, Ricardo makes the same point:

> The aggregate capitals will be increased! Now if labour cannot be procured no more work will be done with additional capital, but wages will rise, and the distribution of the produce will be favourable to the workmen. In this case no more food will be produced if the workmen were well fed before, their demand will be for conveniences, and luxuries (1951, VIII, p. 258).

There is no suggestion in any of these passages that prices will rise to offset the increases in money wages to leave the real wages bill unchanged. On the contrary, workers can and do become better off by increasing their consumption of luxuries and other enjoyments. Another important dissident from the McCulloch line was J.S. Mill himself and we will be examining his approach in the next section.

It appears then that McCulloch may justifiably be regarded as the founder of the wages fund doctrine in Lakatosian terms if no other. Thus it was not merely because he presented an arithmetical example that his version was more rigid but because it was logically more robust. Of course, the lemma that was implicitly added by McCulloch was open to the criticism that it lacked realism, but this could have been defended on the analytical ground that some assumptions have to be made about behaviour in different sectors of the economy, and on the empirical ground that luxury consumption was only likely to be a very small part of workers' total consumption. By contrast, in not adopting this lemma consistently the Classical economists were being more realistic and more optimistic in allowing for a growth in the standards of living of ordinary workers, but were leaving the wages fund doctrine open to attack on the grounds that money funds were flexible even if real funds were fixed. Significantly, it was on these very grounds that Mill recanted from the doctrine in 1869.

J.S. Mill, money and the recantation

J.S. Mill's analysis of the effects of increasing money allocations to labour is very interesting and at odds with the approach advocated by McCulloch – nowhere more so, of course, than in the recantation itself. At one point he appears to be supporting the McCulloch line. In book I chapter IV of the *Principles* on 'Capital', he is considering the case of a hardware manufacturer who hypothetically switches a large sum of expenditure from plate and jewels to productive labourers:

> The labourers, on receiving their increased wages, will not lay them out in plate and jewels, but in food. There is not, however, additional food in the country; nor any unproductive labourers or animals, as in the former case, whose food is set free for productive purposes. Food will therefore be imported if possible; if not possible, the labourers will remain for a season on their short allowance (1871, pp. 55–6).

Workers then receive increased money wages which with a fixed stock of wage goods and *no imports* will leave workers on the same real wage. Presumably goods prices will rise to perfectly offset the increase in money wages although Mill does not say this. This is an interesting example because it presumes that where workers are not fully supplied with the necessaries of life, increased money wages will be directed towards consumption of necessaries exclusively, forcing their prices up. In other words, consumption of luxuries by workers in this state is ruled out. Here Mill *is* making use of the hard core 'McCulloch version' of the wages fund doctrine and again as with McCulloch the price changes necessary to reconcile money and real versions are implicit, not explicit.

When we turn to his discussion of the first proposition on capital, however, a different picture emerges. Here Mill turns his attention to the argument, which he very strongly opposed, that unproductive consumption by the rich is necessary for the poor. On the contrary, Mill argued, all acts of investments by capitalists involving transfers of expenditure from unproductive to productive activity will benefit either the income or employment levels of the workers. Opponents of this view would argue that demand by capitalists will have fallen and thus the increased output by productive workers will remain unsold. But, Mill argues, this is not the whole story:

> In the case supposed, there would no longer be any demand for luxuries, on the part of capitalists and landowners. But when these classes turn their income into capital, they do not thereby annihilate their power of consumption; they transfer it from themselves to the labourers to whom they give employment. Now, there are two possible suppositions in regard to the labourers; either there is or there is not, an increase of their numbers, proportional to the increase of capital. If there is, the case offers no difficulty. The production of necessaries for the new population, takes the place of the production of luxuries for a portion of the old, and supplied exactly the

amount of employment which has been lost. But suppose that there is not increase of population. The whole of what was previously expended in luxuries, by capitalists and landlords, is distributed among the existing labourers, in the form of additional wages. We will assume them to be already sufficiently supplied with necessaries. What follows? That the labourers become consumers of luxuries; and the capital previously employed in the production of luxuries is still able to employ itself in the same manner: the difference being, that the luxuries are shared among the community generally, instead of being confined to a few (1871, pp. 67–8).

This is very important passage. Here Mill is arguing that in the case of a fixed labour supply the workers are assumed, unlike in the earlier example, to have all the necessaries they require. Increases in the money funds will not simply be offset by rising wage goods prices because there is no added competition for such commodities. Instead workers can use their increased money (and real) incomes to purchase luxury goods. It is interesting to note that it is only when workers are fully 'supported with necessaries' that they will attempt to consume luxuries. Mill imagines a hierarchy of goods and, while consumption of the higher level luxuries by workers is allowed for, it is only when their more basic needs are being met. Mill, it seems, believed that workers' consumption of luxury goods depended upon their level of real income and did not assume a rigid separation of workers' and capitalists' consumption. Further support for this approach is found in book IV, chapter II where Mill outlines his long run wage analysis. Improved technology may lower prices and when prices fell:

> ... of those goods which labourers generally do not consume ... all who consume them, whether landlords, capitalists, *or skilled and privileged labourers*, obtain increased means of enjoyment ... The landlords and the *privileged classes of labourers*, if they are consumers of the same commodities, share the same benefit (1871, pp. 715–16).

This quotation reinforces Mill's general approach suggesting that some better off sections of the workforce – who are presumably well fed or sufficiently supplied with necessaries – can and do consume luxuries.

Against this background, it is not surprising that Mill took the line he did in the recantation, where he argued that the money funds available to the capitalist for the payment of wages were 'co-extensive with the whole proceeds of his business, after keeping up his machinery, buildings and materials and feeding his family' (1869, p. 517) and could be bargained for by the workforce. Ekelund (1976) has criticized Mill for failing to realize that *any* increase in money allocations to labour will trigger offsetting rises in goods prices given zero crossovers in consumption between capitalists' and workers' goods – the McCulloch approach. But Mill would not wish to incorporate the lemma required for this strategy. He had already argued *for* consumption cross-overs in 1848 and, although he rather disingenuously criticizes himself in the recantation for taking the orthodox view of the wages fund doctrine, it is clear that he held a rather sophisticated view of the relationship between real wages, workers' consumption behaviour and prices. It seems likely that external factors played an important role in prompting Mill to recant from the wages fund doctrine (see Vint (1981)) but the doctrine was theoretically problematic from the beginning and Mill's recantation was based on theoretical grounds. He could not reconcile the existence of flexible money funds with the rigid requirements of the doctrine, and the ubiquitous 'monster of money' which McCulloch attempted to vanquish in 1825 finally triumphed in 1869.

Conclusions

With hindsight and viewed through Lakatosian spectacles it is clear that, when faced with the real versus money wages fund dichotomy, the options open to the Classical economists to deal with the problem were very limited. As we have already argued, monster-barring, monster-adjustment and exception-barring were not really feasible given the importance of money, and this left three real choices.

First, they could have adopted the McCulloch approach, which we have argued here is an example of Lakatosian lemma incorporation, and, having done this, sought to defend a more limited but more robust theorem. It has been shown in this chapter that this was *not* done and that writers such as Ricardo and J.S. Mill did wish to allow for the possibility that workers' real living standards could rise in *the short run* as well as the long as a result of increased money wage payments.

Secondly, they could have attempted lemma replacement and sought a theoretical amendment to the doctrine that would deal with the money problem. We know that this also did not happen and it may well be impossible. It is difficult to conceive of a simple theoretical amendment to the doctrine which could both preserve the existing rigidity and yet allow for the flexibility of money funds.

The third and final option available was surrender, leading to the abandonment of the doctrine and ultimately this is, of course, what happened. Mill surrendered in 1869 but, as Lakatos himself would predict, the existence of an undefeated counter-example would not lead to abandonment in the absence of a superior alternative. The fact that there was no such alternative explains both Cairnes's attempt to revive the doctrine and Mill's efforts to minimize the damage in the last edition of the *Principles* in 1871 where he conceded that workers may be able to raise wages at the expense of profits but that their power to do so was very limited.

Notes

1. O'Brien himself argues that Marcet was probably the author of the wages fund doctrine, although in saying this he is probably following Cannan (1970, p. 360).

2. See, for example, Hollander (1968), Ekelund (1976), West and Hafer (1978), Vint (1981) and Negishi (1986).
3. For a powerful argument in favour of using Lakatos's approach for historical but not heuristic purposes, see Feyerabend (1976).
4. Fulton cites Lakatos's references to Newton's laws of gravity and Bohr's five postulates on energy emission in simple atomic systems (see Fulton (1984, p. 189) and Lakatos (1970, p. 133).
5. See Fulton (1984, pp. 191–4) for further discussion on this point and Leijonhufvud (1976) for a similar view.
6. I have almost completed a larger study of Classical wage theory undertaken from a Lakatosian perspective. It is clear that in the work of the earlier writers such as Smith, Malthus and Ricardo the hard core is not fully developed and only becomes so in the work of Marcet and McCulloch. Notwithstanding the theoretical difficulties with the doctrine, it appears to have made some Lakatosian theoretical progress in the 1830s and 1840s measured in terms of the production of novel facts. See Vint (1986) for a preliminary discussion.
7. See Vint (1986).
8. My emphasis.
9. McCulloch is less clear on this point in later editions. Thus in the 1849 edition when discussing the ability of a country to support workers he simply refers to 'amount of its wealth, or of its capital applicable to the employment of labour' [1849, p. 397].
10. Harriet Martineau, for example, in 'The Manchester Strike', (the seventh of the *Illustrations of Political Economy*, series published in 1832–34) used the wages fund doctrine to argue that strikes are futile and in doing so made exactly the same point that McCulloch does about the relationship of money and real wages. See Martineau (1832, p. 57).

References

Blaug, M. (1976), 'Kuhn Versus Lakatos or Paradigms versus Research Programmes in the History of Economic Thought', in S.J. Latsis, (ed.), *Method and Appraisal in Economics*, Cambridge: Cambridge University Press.

Blaug, M. (1980), *The Methodology of Economics*, Cambridge: Cambridge University Press.

Bonar, J. (1885), *Malthus and His Work*, (reprinted in 1924 from a copy printed by Clay and Sons), New York: Allen and Unwin.

Cannan, E. (1893), *A History of the Theories of Production and Distribution*, London: Percival and Co.

Ekelund, R.B. (1976), 'A Short Run Classical Model of Capital and Wages: Mill's Recantation of the Wages Fund', *Oxford Economic Papers*, **28**, (1), March, pp. 66–86.

Feyerabend, P. (1976), 'On the Critique of Scientific Reason', in R.S. Cohen, P.K. Feyerabend, and M.W. Wartofsky, (eds), *Essays in Honour of Imre Lakatos*, Boston Studies in the Philosophy of Science, Vol XXXIX, Boston: D. Reidel.

Fisher, R.M. (1986), *The Logic of Economic Discovery: Neoclassical Economics and the Marginal Revolution*, Brighton: Wheatsheaf.

Fulton, G. (1984), 'Research Programmes in Economics', *History of Political Economy*, **16** (2), pp. 187–205.

Hollander, S. (1968), 'The Role of Fixed Technical Coefficients in the Evolution of the Wages Fund Controversy', *Oxford Economic Papers*, **20**, (3), November, pp. 320–41.

Lakatos, I. (1970), 'Falsification and the Methodology of Scientific Research Programmes', in I. Lakatos and A. Musgrave, *Criticism and the Growth of Knowledge*, Cambridge: Cambridge University Press.

Lakatos, I. (1976), *Proofs and Refutations*, Cambridge: Cambridge University Press.

Latsis, S. (1976), 'A Research Programme in Economics', in Latsis, S.J. (ed), *Method and Appraisal in Economics*, Cambridge: Cambridge University Press.

Leijonhufvud, A. (1976), 'Schools, "Revolutions", and Research Programmes in Economic Theory', in S.J. Latsis, (ed.), *Method and Appraisal in Economics*, Cambridge: Cambridge University Press.

de Marchi, N. (1976), 'Anomaly and the Development of Economics: the Case of the Leontief Paradox', in S.J. Latsis, (ed.) *Method and Appraisal in Economics*, Cambridge: Cambridge University Press, pp. 109–27.

Martineau, H. (1832), 'The Manchester Strike', *Illustrations of Political Economy*, no. 7, London: Charles Fox.

McCulloch, J.R. (1825), *Principles of Political Economy*, London: Ward, Lock & Co.

McCulloch, J.R. (1826), *An Essay on the Circumstances which Determine the Rate of Wages and the Condition of the Labouring Classes*, Edinburgh, (reprinted and revised as a Treatise, London, 1851 and 1854).

Mill, J.S. (1871), *Principles of Political Economy*, London: J.W. Parker. (First edition, 1848.)

Mill, J.S. (1869), 'Thornton on Labour and its Claims', *Fortnightly Review*, May, June, pp. 505–18, 680–700.

Negishi, T. (1986), 'Thornton's Criticism of Equilibrium Theory and Mill', *History of Political Economy*, **18** (4), pp. 567–77.

O'Brien, D.P. (1970), *J.R. McCulloch: A Study in Classical Economics*, London: Allen and Unwin.

O'Brien, D.P. (1976), 'The Longevity of Adam Smith's Vision: Paradigms, Research Programmes and Falsifiability in the History of Economic Thought', *Scottish Journal of Political Economy*, **XXIII**, (2) June, pp. 133–51.

Ricardo, D. (1817), *Principles of Political Economy*, edited by P. Sraffa, (1951–55) London: Cambridge University Press.

Schumpeter, J.A. (1954), *History of Economic Analysis*, New York: Allen and Unwin.

Vint, J. (1981), 'A Two Sector Model of the Wages Fund: Mill's Recantation Revisited', *British Review of Economic Issues*, **3**, (9), Autumn.

Vint, J. (1986), 'Research Programmes and the Classical Theory of Wages: A Case Study', *History of Economics Society Conference Papers*, New York: Columbia University.

West, E.G. and Hafer, R.W. (1978), 'J. S. Mill, Unions and the Wages Fund Recantation: A Reinterpretation', *Q. J. E.*, **XCII**, (4), pp. 603–19.

PART III

ASPECTS OF CLASSICAL CONTROVERSIES OVER MONEY AND BANKING

7 Kaldor versus Friedman in historical perspective

Thomas M. Humphrey

Introduction

The rise of Milton Friedman's version of monetarism in the 1960s and early 1970s provoked an antimonetarist backlash culminating in the late Nicholas Kaldor's *The Scourge of Monetarism* (1982). Friedman stressed the ideas of exogenous (that is, central bank determined) money, money-to-price causality, inflation as a monetary phenomenon, and controllability of money through the high-powered monetary base.[1] He traced a chain of causation running from open market operations to bank reserves to the nominal stock of money and thence to aggregate spending, nominal income, and prices.

By contrast, Kaldor postulated the opposite notions of endogenous (that is, demand-determined) money, reverse causality, and inflation as a cost-push or supply-shock phenomenon.[2] He denied the possibility of base control given the central bank's responsibility to guarantee bank liquidity and the financial sector's ability to engineer changes in the turnover velocity of money via the manufacture of money substitutes. Kaldor's transmission mechanism runs from wages (and other factor costs) to prices to money and thence to bank reserves. Wages determine prices, prices influence loan demands, and loan demands via their accommodation in the form of new checking deposits created by commercial banks determine the money stock, with central banks passively supplying the necessary reserves.

Kaldor claimed his attack on monetarism was in the tradition of Keynes's *General Theory* – so much so that he labelled it 'a Keynesian perspective on money'.[3] In so doing, he contributed to the standard textbook tendency to treat the monetarist–antimonetarist debate as a post-Keynesian development. This chapter shows that the debate long predates Keynes, that it is rooted in classical monetary tradition, and that it traces back at least to the bullionist–antibullionist and currency school–banking school disputes in England in the nineteenth century. More precisely, the following paragraphs demonstrate that the arguments of Friedman and Kaldor were fully anticipated by their classical predecessors.

Bullionist controversy (1797–1821)

Monetarism did not begin with Friedman nor did antimonetarism originate with Kaldor or Keynes's *General Theory*. Those doctrines clashed as early as the Bank Restriction period of the Napoleonic wars when the Bank of England suspended the convertibility of its notes into gold at a fixed price on demand.[4] The suspension of specie payments and the resulting move to inconvertible paper was followed by a rise in the paper pound price of commodities, gold bullion, and foreign currencies. A debate between strict bullionists, moderate bullionists, and antibullionists then arose over the question, 'Was there inflation in England and if so what was its cause?'[5]

Strict bullionists: the classical monetarists

Led by David Ricardo, the strict bullionists argued that inflation did exist, that over-issue of banknotes by the Bank of England was the cause, and that the premium on gold (the difference between the market and official mint price of gold in terms of paper money) together with the pound's depreciation on the foreign exchange constituted the proof. Price index numbers not then being in general use, the bullionists used the gold premium and depreciated exchange rate to measure inflation.

The bullionists arrived at their conclusions via the following route. The Bank of England determines the quantity of inconvertible paper money. The quantity of money via its impact on aggregate spending determines domestic prices. Domestic prices, given foreign prices, determine the exchange rate so as to equalize worldwide the common-currency price of goods. Finally, the exchange rate between inconvertible paper and gold standard currencies determines the paper premium on specie so as to equalize everywhere the gold price of goods. In short, causality runs unidirectionally from money to prices to the exchange rate and the gold premium. It followed that the depreciation of the exchange rate below gold parity (that is, below the ratio of the respective mint prices of gold in each country) together with the premium on specie constituted evidence that prices were higher and the quantity of money greater in England than would have been the case had convertibility reigned. Here is a straightforward application of the monetarist ideas of exogenous money, money-to-price causality, inflation as a monetary phenomenon, and purchasing power parity.[6] On these grounds the strict bullionists attributed depreciation of the internal and external value of the pound solely to the redundancy of money and reproached the Bank for having taken advantage of the suspension of convertibility to over-issue the currency.

The strict bullionists also enunciated the monetarist notion of control of the money stock through the high-powered monetary base. With respect to base control, they argued that the Bank of England could, through its own note issue, regulate the note issue of the country (non-London) banks as well as other privately issued means of payment (bills of exchange and checking deposits). Two circumstances, they said, worked to ensure base controllability. First, country banks tended to hold in reserve Bank of England notes (or balances with London agents transferable into such notes) equal to a relatively fixed fraction of their own note liabilities. This established a constant relationship between the Bank note base and the country note component of the money stock. Second, a fixed exchange rate regional balance of payments or specie-flow mechanism kept country bank notes in line with the Bank's own issues. Country bank notes were fully convertible into Bank of England notes but did not circulate in London. Should country banks over-issue, the resulting rise in local prices over London prices would lead to a demand to convert local currency into Bank of England notes to make cheaper purchases in London. The ensuing drain on reserves would force country banks to contract their note issue, thus eliminating the excess. For these reasons, the quantity of country notes was tied by a rigid link to the volume of Bank notes and could only expand and contract with the latter.[7] The implication was clear: Bank of England notes drove the entire money stock. Country banks were exonerated as a source of inflation.

The strict bullionists displayed another monetarist trait in prescribing rules rather than discretion in the conduct of monetary policy. Their rule called for the Bank of England to contract its note issue upon the first sign of exchange depreciation or rise in the price of gold. This rule derived from the famous *Ricardian definition of excess* according to which if the exchange was depreciated and gold was commanding a premium the currency was by definition excessive and should be contracted.[8]

Moderate bullionists

Moderate bullionists, led by Henry Thornton, Thomas Malthus, and William Blake, modified the strict bullionists' analysis in one respect: they argued that it applied to the long run, but not necessarily to the short. They held that in the short run real as well as monetary shocks could affect the exchange rate such that temporary depreciation did not necessarily signify monetary over-issue. In the long run, however, real shocks were self-correcting and only monetary disturbances remained. Their position is best exemplified by Blake's distinction between the *real* and *nominal* exchanges. The real exchange or barter terms of trade, he said, registers the impact of nonmonetary disturbances – crop failures, unilateral transfers, trade embargoes and the like – to the balance of payments. By contrast, the nominal exchange reflects the relative purchasing powers of foreign and domestic currencies as determined by their relative supplies. Both components contribute to exchange rate movements in the short run. In the long run, however, the real exchange is self-correcting (that is, it returns to its natural equilibrium level) and only the nominal exchange can remain permanently depressed. Therefore, persistent exchange depreciation is a sure sign of monetary over-issue.[9] On this point the moderate bullionists agreed with their strict bullionist colleagues.

Antibullionists: the classical nonmonetarists

Opposed to the bullionists were the antibullionist defenders of the Bank of England. They denied that the Bank had over-issued or that domestic monetary policy had anything to do with the depreciating exchange rate and rising price of gold. Such inflationary symptoms they attributed to real rather than monetary causes. In so doing, they contributed two key ideas that today appear in Kaldor's work.

First was their supply-shock or cost-push theory of inflation. They argued that crop failures and wartime disturbances to foreign trade had raised the price of wheat and other staple foodstuffs that constituted the main component of workers' budgets. These price increases then passed through into money wages and thus raised the price of all goods produced by labour. Ricardo, however, convincingly replied that this explanation confused relative with absolute prices. For without excessive money growth, a rise in the relative price of wheat that required workers to spend more on that commodity would leave them with less to spend on other goods whose prices would accordingly fall. In that case the rise in the price of wheat would be offset by compensating falls in other relative prices leaving general prices unchanged.

Second, the antibullionists enunciated the notion of an endogenous, demand-determined money stock. This came in the form of their *real bills doctrine*, which they employed to assert the impossibility of an excess supply of money ever developing to spill over into the commodity market to put upward pressure on prices. The real bills doctrine states that money can never be excessive if issued upon the discount of sound, short-term commercial bills drawn to finance real goods in the process of production and distribution. It purports to match money creation with real output so that no inflation occurs.[10]

The antibullionists used this idea to defend the Bank of England against the charge that it had caused inflation through over-issue. The Bank, they said, was blameless since it had restricted its issues to real bills of exchange and so had merely responded to the real needs of trade. In other words, the Bank, by limiting its advances to commercial paper representing actual output, had merely responded to a loan demand for money already in existence and had done nothing inflationary to create that demand.

The real bills doctrine was an early version of Kaldor's notion that a passive, demand-determined money stock cannot be over-issued and so cannot cause inflation.[11] Antibullionists also anticipated Kaldor in arguing that since no one would borrow at interest money not needed, the Bank could not force an excess issue on the market. Such excess, they said, would be speedily extinguished as borrowers returned it to the Bank to pay off costly loans. In short, the antibullionists held that the Bank could not cause inflation since it merely supplied money passively in response to a loan demand for it. Thus there could be no excess issue to spill over into the commodity market in the form of an excess demand for goods to bid up prices.

Critique of the real bills doctrine

Monetarists today criticize Kaldor's notion of a transmission mechanism running unidirectionally from wages to prices to money for ignoring the feedback effect of money on prices. Adding this feedback loop produces a two-way interaction in which prices and money can chase each other upward *ad infinitum* in a self-reinforcing inflationary spiral. Monetarists argue that such a spiral is sure to result if banks, in passively creating new money in response to loan demands for it, set the loan rate of interest below the expected rate of profit on the use of the borrowed funds. In this case loan demands will be insatiable and the resulting rise in money and prices will be without limit.[12]

Bullionists, especially Henry Thornton, advanced exactly this same argument against the antibullionists' real bills doctrine. That doctrine, they said, suffers from two basic flaws. First, it links the nominal money stock with the nominal volume of bills, a variable that moves in step with prices and thus the money stock itself. In so doing it renders the latter two variables indeterminate.[13] It thus ensures that any inadvertent jump in money and prices will, by raising the nominal value of goods in the process of production and hence the nominal quantity of bills eligible for discount, lead to further increases in money and prices *ad infinitum* in a self-justifying inflationary spiral. Second, it overlooks the fact that the demand for loans and volume of bills offered for discount depends not so much on real output to be financed, as on the perceived profitability of borrowing as indicated by the differential between the loan rate of interest and the expected rate of profit on the use of the borrowed funds. In particular, it fails to see that when the profit rate exceeds the loan rate the demand for loans becomes insatiable and the real bills criterion fails to limit the quantity of money in existence.[14]

This last flaw, bullionists argued, rendered the real bills doctrine an especially dangerous policy guide under inconvertibility. To be sure, even under specie convertibility a central bank that set its loan rate too low relative to the expected profit rate would find itself inundated with a potentially unlimited supply of eligible bills clamouring for discount. But the resulting rise in money and prices would, by making home goods dearer than foreign ones, lead to a trade deficit and a matching gold drain that would force the bank to protect its metallic reserves by raising its loan rate, thereby ending the inflation. No such result was assured under paper currency regimes, however. For without the crucial check of convertibility, the profit rate–loan rate differential could persist indefinitely and with it the self-reinforcing rise in money, prices, and commercial bills. This point was particularly telling during the suspension period when usury ceilings constrained the Bank of England's lending rate to 5 per cent at a time when the expected profit rate, buoyed by the boom conditions of the Napoleonic wars, was well in excess of that level.

Currency school–banking school debate (1821–1845)

Monetarist and antimonetarist doctrines clashed again in the three decades following the Bank of England's restoration of the gold convertibility of its notes in 1821. This time the debate focused on how to protect the currency from over-issue so as to secure the gold reserve and ensure the maintenance of convertibility. The protagonists in this dispute were known collectively as the currency school and the banking school, but they were the intellectual heirs of the bullionists and antibullionists.[15] Leaders of the currency school included Samuel Jones Loyd (Lord Overstone), George Warde Norman, and Robert Torrens. Thomas Tooke, John Fullarton, James Wilson, and J.B. Gilbart led the banking school.[16]

The currency school's bullionist predecessors had assumed that a convertible currency needed no protection. If the currency were convertible, they reasoned, any excess issue of notes which raised British prices relative to foreign prices would be converted into gold to make cheaper purchases abroad. The resulting loss of specie reserves would immediately force the Bank to contract its note issue thus quickly arresting the drain and restoring the money stock and prices to their pre-existing equilibrium levels. Given smooth and rapid adjustment (monetary self-correction), convertibility was its own safeguard.

A series of monetary crises in the 1820s and 1830s, however, convinced the currency school that adjustment was far from smooth and that convertibility *per se* was not a guaranteed safeguard to over-issue. It was an inadequate safeguard because it allowed banks – commercial and central – too much discretion in the management of their note issue. Banks could and did continue to issue notes even as gold was flowing out, delaying contraction until the last possible minute, and then contracting with a violence that sent shock waves throughout the economy.

Currency school's prescription

What was needed, the currency school thought, was a law removing the note issue from the discretion of bankers and placing it under strict regulation. To be effective, this law should require the banking system to contract its note issue one-for-one with outflows of gold so as to put a gradual and early stop to specie drains. Such a law would embody the currency school's *principle of metallic fluctuation* according to which a mixed currency of paper and coin should be made to behave exactly as if it were wholly metallic, automatically expanding and contracting to match inflows and outflows of gold.[17] Departure from this rule, the currency school argued, would permit persistent over-issue of paper, forcing an efflux of specie through the balance of payments, which in turn would endanger the gold reserve, threaten gold convertibility, compel the need for sharp contraction, and thereby precipitate financial panics. Such panics would be exacerbated if internal gold drains coincided with external ones, as moneyholders, alarmed by the possibility of suspension, sought to convert paper currency into gold. No such consequences would ensue, however, if the currency conformed to the metallic principle. Forced to behave like gold (regarded by the currency school as the stablest of monetary standards) the currency would be spared those sharp procyclical fluctuations in quantity that constitute a prime source of economic disturbance.

The currency school scored a triumph when its ideas were enacted into law. The Bank Charter Act of 1844 embodied its prescription that, except for a small fixed fiduciary issue, Bank notes were to be backed by an identical amount of gold while the country bank note issue was frozen at its 1842 level. In modern terminology, the Act effectively established a marginal gold reserve requirement of 100 per cent behind note issues. With notes tied to gold in this fashion, their volume would start to shrink as soon as specie drains signalled the earliest appearance of over-issue. Monetary over-expansion would be corrected automatically before it could do much damage.

Banking school
The rival banking school flatly rejected the currency school's prescription of mandatory 100 per cent gold cover for notes. Indeed, the banking school denied the need for statutory note control of any kind, arguing that a convertible note issue was automatically regulated by the needs of trade and required no further limitation. This conclusion stemmed directly from the real bills doctrine and *law of reflux*, which the banking school took from the antibullionists and applied to convertible currency regimes.

The school's real bills doctrine stated that money could never be excessive if issued on loans made to finance real transactions in goods and services. Similarly the law of reflux asserted that over-issue was impossible because any excess notes would be returned instantaneously to the banks for conversion into coin or for repayment of loans. Both doctrines embodied the notions of a passive, demand-determined money supply and of reverse causality running from economic activity and prices to money rather than vice versa as in the currency school's view. According to the reverse causality hypothesis, changes in the level of prices and production induce corresponding shifts in the demand for bank loans which the banks accommodate via variations in the note issue. In this way prices help determine the note component of the money stock, the expansion of which is the result, not the cause, of price inflation. As for the price level itself, the banking school attributed its determination to factor incomes or costs (wages, interest, rents, and so on) thus establishing the essentials of a cost-push theory of inflation. The importance of the cost-push idea to the banking school cannot be overestimated: it even led Thomas Tooke to argue that high-interest-rate tight-money policies were inflationary since they raised the interest component of business costs.[18]

Antimonetarist ideas

The concepts of cost inflation, reverse causality and passive money are the hallmarks of an extreme antimonetarist view of the monetary transmission mechanism to which the banking school adhered. Its list of anti-monetarist ideas also included the propositions:

1. that international gold movements are absorbed by and released from idle hoards and have no effect on the volume of money in circulation
2. that an efflux of specie stems from real shocks to the balance of payments and not from domestic price inflation
3. that changes in the stock of money tend to be offset by compensating changes in the stock of money substitutes leaving the total circulation unchanged
4. that discretion is superior to rules in the conduct of monetary policy.

In its critique of the monetarist doctrines of the currency school, which contended that note over-issue is the root cause of domestic inflation and specie drains, the banking school argued as follows: Over-issue is impossible since the stock of notes is determined by the needs of trade and cannot exceed demand. Therefore, no excess supply of money exists to spill over into the goods market to bid up prices. In any case, causality runs from real activity and prices to money rather than vice versa. Finally, specie drains stem from real rather than monetary disturbances and occur independently of domestic price level movements.

These arguments severed all but one of the links in the currency school's monetary transmission mechanism running from money to prices to the trade balance, thence to specie flows and their impact on the high-powered monetary base and finally back again to money. The final link was broken when the banking school asserted that gold flows come from idle hoards (that is, buffer stocks of specie reserves) and could not affect the volume of money in circulation. Falling solely on the hoards, gold drains would find their monetary effects neutralized (sterilized) by the implied fall in reserve-note and reserve-deposit ratios. To ensure that these hoards would be sufficient to accommodate gold drains, the banking school recommended that the Bank of England hold larger metallic reserves. With regard to the currency school's prescription that discretionary policy be replaced by a fixed rule, the banking school rejected it on the grounds that rigid rules would prevent the banking system from responding to the needs of trade and would hamper the central bank's power to deal with financial crises. Finally, the banking school asserted the impossibility of controlling the entire stock of money and money substitutes through the bank note component alone, since limitation of notes would simply induce the public to use money substitutes (deposits and bills of exchange) instead. In other words, the total circulation is like a balloon; when squeezed at one end, it expands at the other. More generally, the banking school questioned the efficacy of base control in a financial system that could generate an endless supply of money substitutes.

The currency school, however, rejected this criticism on the grounds that the volume of deposits and bills was rigidly constrained by the volume of notes and therefore could be controlled through notes alone. In short, the total circulation was like an inverted pyramid resting on a bank note base, with variations in the base inducing equiproportional variations in the superstructure of money substitutes. In counting deposits as part of the superstructure, the currency school excluded them from its concept of money. It did so on the grounds that deposits, unlike notes and coin, were not generally acceptable in final payments during financial crises.

Subsequent developments

In retrospect, the currency school erred in failing to define deposits as money to be regulated like notes. This failure enabled the Bank of England to exercise discretionary control over a large and growing part of the money stock, contrary to the intentions of the school. The school also erred in not recognizing the need for a lender of last resort to avert liquidity panics and domestic specie drains. With respect to specie drains, the currency school refused to distinguish between domestic (internal) and foreign (external) ones. As far as policy was concerned, both drains were to be handled the same way, namely by monetary contraction. By the time Walter Bagehot wrote his celebrated *Lombard Street* in 1873, however, it was widely recognized that the two drains required different treatment and that the surest way to arrest an internal drain was through a policy of liberal lending. Such drains were caused by panic-induced demands for high-powered money (gold and Bank notes) and could be terminated by the central bank's announced readiness to satiate those demands.[19] The currency school nevertheless remained opposed to such a policy, fearing it would place too much discretionary power in the hands of the central bank. These shortcomings in no way invalidated the currency school's contention that convertibility is an inadequate safeguard to over-issue and therefore must be reinforced by positive regulation. Nor did they undermine its monetary theory of inflation, which was superior to any explanation its critics had to offer.

As for the banking school, it rightly stressed the importance of checking deposits in the payments mechanism. But it was wrong in insisting that the real bills doctrine, which tied note issues to loans made for productive purposes, would prevent inflationary money growth. The currency school triumphantly exposed this flaw by pointing out that rising prices would require an ever-growing volume of loans just to finance the same level of real transactions. In this way inflation would justify the monetary expansion necessary to sustain it and the real bills criterion would fail to limit the quantity of money in existence. Also, by the 1890s Knut Wicksell had rigorously demonstrated the same point made by Henry Thornton in 1802, namely that an insatiable demand for loans results when the loan rate of interest is below the expected rate of profit on capital.[20] In such cases the real bills criterion provides no bar to over-issue.

Despite this criticism the real bills doctrine survived in banking tradition to be incorporated as a key concept in the Federal Reserve Act of 1913. And during the German hyperinflation of 1922–23 the doctrine formed the basis of the Reichsbank's policy of issuing astronomical sums of money to satisfy the needs of trade at ever-rising prices. Oblivious to the Thornton–Wicksell demonstration that the real bills test provides no check to over-issue when lenders peg loan rates below the going profit rate, the Reichsbank insisted on pegging its discount rate at 12 per cent (later raised to 90 per cent) at a time when the going market rate of interest was well in excess of 7000 per cent per annum.[21] This huge differential of course made it extremely profitable for commercial banks to rediscount bills with the Reichsbank and to loan out the proceeds, thereby producing additional inflationary expansion of the money supply and further upward pressure on interest rates. The authorities failed to perceive this inflationary sequence and did nothing to stop it. On the contrary, they saw their duty as passively supplying on demand the growing sums of money required to mediate real transactions at skyrocketing prices. They simply refused to believe that issuing money on loan against genuine commercial bills could have an inflationary effect.

After the hyperinflation débâcle of the 1920s, banking school doctrines reappeared in renovated form as part of the Keynesian revolution. Keynes in his *General Theory* (1936) stressed the banking school's notion of money entering idle hoards (liquidity traps) rather than active circulation. He also stressed the school's ideas:

1. of variable velocity absorbing the impact of money–stock changes leaving spending and prices unaffected
2. of real rather than monetary causes of cyclical depressions
3. of prices determined by autonomous factor costs.

And in the immediate post-war period, Keynesians developed the notion of cost-push inflation emanating from growing union bargaining strength, business monopoly power, supply shortages, and other institutional forces that produce autonomous increases in labour and other factor costs. Only the banking school ideas of unlimited money substitutes and the futility of base control were missing. And these were provided in the famous report of the British Radcliffe Committee (1959). Representing the apogee of post-Keynesian scepticism of the relevancy of the quantity theory, the Radcliffe Report concluded that attempts to control inflation by limiting the stock of a narrowly defined monetary aggregate would merely induce spenders to turn to money substitutes instead.[22] Velocity would rise to offset monetary restriction.

The debate goes on
Today currency school doctrines survive in Friedman's work just as banking school doctrines appear in Kaldor's writings. When Friedman argues that rules are preferable to discretion, that inflation is largely or solely the result of excessive monetary growth, that monetary shocks are a primary cause of cyclical swings, and that the entire stock of money and money substitutes can be governed by control of the high-powered monetary base, he echoes currency school opinion.

Likewise, Kaldor echoes the doctrines of the banking school. The school's cost-push theory informs his view of inflation. Inflation, he argues, stems mainly from increasing militancy of trade unions and the resulting rise in unit labour costs caused by money wages advancing faster than labour-hour productivity.[23] The banking school's notion of passive money appears in his statement that money is a demand-determined variable that comes into existence as banks accommodate loan demands and central banks acting as lenders of last resort permissively supply the necessary reserves.[24] The school's law of reflux surfaces in his declaration that because money is demand-determined its supply can never exceed demand; any oversupply is extinguished automatically as borrowers return it to the banks to pay off costly loans.[25] Finally, the banking school notion of a potentially unlimited supply of money substitutes underlies his belief in the futility of base control. Like the banking school, he argues that restriction of the monetary base induces offsetting rises in the stock of money substitutes thereby thwarting base control.[26]

In short, Kaldor emerges as the intellectual heir of the banking school and the antibullionists just as Friedman is the heir of the currency school and the bullionists. It follows that the debate between the monetarists and antimonetarists is not of post-Keynesian origin. Rather it has its roots in policy controversies going back to the era of classical monetary thought.

Notes
1. See Friedman (1970, pp. 22–8) for his statement of the basic propositions of monetarism.

2. Kaldor's antimonetarist views are conveniently summarized in Chapter 3 of Thirlwall (1988).
3. See the article of that same title by Kaldor and Trevithick (1981).
4. In fact, the doctrines had clashed at least once before in Sweden in the mid-1700s. On this earlier debate see Eagly (1968, 1971).
5. On the bullionist controversy see the classic accounts of Viner (1937), Fetter (1965), Mints (1945), and Schumpeter (1954). For recent interpretations see O'Brien (1975), Laidler (1987), and Humphrey (1974).
6. Formally, the strict bullionist analysis reduces to a simple three-equation model linking goods prices P, money stock M, exchange rate E, and gold price P_g. Using asterisks to distinguish foreign currency variables from those denominated in home currency, the model is:

$$P = kM$$

$$E = P/P^* = P/1 = P$$

$$P_g = EP_g^* = E \cdot 1 = E.$$

The first equation embodies the crude quantity theory of money according to which domestic prices P are a fixed fraction k of the domestic money stock M. The second equation defines the equilibrium or purchasing power parity exchange rate E as the ratio of domestic to foreign goods prices P/P^*. For simplicity, foreign prices are taken as given and normalized at unity. The final equation defines the paper pound price of gold P_g as the product of the exchange rate E and the foreign currency price of gold P^*_g. Assuming the foreign country is on the gold standard, the latter variable becomes a fixed constant that, for convenience, is assigned a value of unity.

Substituting the first equation into the second and third yields the expressions:

$$E = kM \text{ and}$$

$$P_g = kM$$

which together state that the exchange rate and the price of gold vary directly and equiproportionally with the money stock. Here is the strict bullionist conclusion that exchange depreciation and the premium on gold indicate an excess issue of money.

7. See Laidler (1987, p. 292) and Morgan (1970, p. 15).
8. On the Ricardian definition of excess see O'Brien (1975, p. 148).
9. Symbolically, Blake's (1810) analysis reduces to $E = RN$, where E is the actual, observed exchange rate, N is the nominal rate expressing relative national price levels as determined by relative national money stocks, and R is the real exchange rate. The latter variable (R) has an equilibrium value of unity determined by the arbitrage condition that the real relative price of goods must be everywhere the same. For details, see Humphrey (1980).
10. On the real bills doctrine and its use by the antibullionists see Humphrey (1982) and the literature there cited.
11. In Kaldor's (1982, p. 70) words, ' ... money comes into existence as a result of borrowing ... from the banks; if as a result of such borrowing, more money comes into existence than the public ... wishes to hold, the excess gets ... repaid to the banks and in this way the "excess money" is extinguished. In technical parlance, the supply of credit money is infinitely elastic at the given rate of interest, and this alone rules out the possibility that an "excess" supply of money ... should be the cause of a "pressure on prices, upwards or downwards".'
12. See, for example, Humphrey (1982).
13. Thornton (1802, pp. 341–2) traced this particular real bills fallacy to John Law, who sought to limit the quantity of paper money by tying it to the nominal value of land.
14. Thornton (1802, pp. 253–4).

15. For classic accounts of the currency school–banking school debate see Viner (1937) and Robbins (1958). For more recent interpretations, see O'Brien (1975), Schwartz (1987), and Humphrey (1974).
16. Both schools were in perfect agreement on the absolute necessity of convertibility and the desirability of the gold standard. What opposition there was to the gold standard came chiefly from the inflationist full-employment-at-any-cost writers of the Birmingham school, notably Thomas Attwood. For details see Humphrey (1977).
17. O'Brien (1975, p. 53) credits the establishment of the metallic principle to Joplin, Drummond, Page, Pennington, and McCulloch.
18. On Tooke's interest cost-push doctrine and its definitive refutation by Knut Wicksell see Humphrey (1979) and the literature there cited.
19. According to Humphrey (1989), Bagehot insisted that such demands be satiated at a penalty rate. The penalty rate would induce borrowers to quickly repay last-resort loans when the crisis was over such that the stock of high-powered money would not long depart from its stable target path.
20. Wicksell developed this point as part of his famous cumulative process model. That Thornton had already enunciated virtually the same model almost 100 years before Wicksell amply confirms Stigler's (1980) adage that no scientific discovery is named for its original discoverer.
21. See Nurkse (1946) and Humphrey (1982).
22. Indeed Cramp (1962) argues convincingly that the Radcliffe Report consists essentially of a modern restatement of the banking school view.
23. See Kaldor and Trevithick (1981, pp. 16–17).
24. Thus Kaldor (1982, p. 47) asserts that 'Precisely because the monetary authorities cannot afford the disastrous consequences of a collapse of the banking system, while the banks in turn cannot allow themselves to get into a position of being "fully stretched", the "money supply"... is *en*dogenous, not *ex*ogenous–it varies in direct response to changes in the public "demand" to hold cash and bank deposits and not independently of that demand'.
25. 'Since .... bank money varies in response to the demand for bank loans ... the supply of money can never be in excess of demand for it; if there was such an excess ... the excess supply would automatically be extinguished through the *repayment* of bank loans ...' see Kaldor (1983, p. 21).
26. See, for example, Kaldor and Trevithick (1981, p. 12) for the argument that 'any attempt to control the supply of the customary forms of money will mean that less customary ways of financing spending will be resorted to, such as trade credit, building society deposits, etc.'

References

Bagehot, W. (1894), *Lombard Street*, New York: Scribner, Armstrong.
Blake, W. (1810), *Observations on the Principles Which Regulate the Course of Exchange; and on the Present Depreciated State of the Currency* (reprinted 1969), New York: Burt Franklin.
Cramp, A.B. (1962), 'Two views on money', *Lloyds Bank Review*, **65**, pp. 1–15.
Eagly, R.V. (1968), 'The Swedish and English bullionist controversies', in R.V. Eagly (ed.), *Events, Ideology, and Economic Theory*, Detroit: Wayne State University Press.
Eagly, R.V. (1971), *The Swedish Bullionist Controversy*, Philadelphia: American Philosophical Society.
Fetter, F.W. (1965), *Development of British Monetary Orthodoxy 1797–1875*, Cambridge: Harvard University Press.
Friedman, M. (1970), *The Counter-Revolution in Monetary Theory*, London: Institute of Economic Affairs.
Humphrey, T.M. (1974), 'The quantity theory of money: its historical evolution and role in policy debates', Federal Reserve Bank of Richmond *Economic Review*, **60**, pp. 2–19; as reprinted in T.M. Humphrey (1986), *Essays on Inflation*, 5th ed., Richmond: Federal Reserve Bank of Richmond, pp. 1–18.
Humphrey, T.M. (1977), 'Two views on monetary policy: the Attwood–Mill debate revisited',

Federal Reserve Bank of Richmond *Economic Review*, **63**, pp. 14–22; as reprinted in Humphrey (1986), pp. 242–50.

Humphrey, T.M. (1979), 'The interest cost-push controversy', Federal Reserve Bank of Richmond *Economic Review*, **65**, pp. 3–10; as reprinted in Humphrey (1986), pp. 143–50.

Humphrey, T.M. (1980), 'Bullionists' exchange rate doctrines and current policy debates', Federal Reserve Bank of Richmond *Economic Review*, **66**, pp. 19–22; as reprinted in Humphrey (1986), pp. 251–4.

Humphrey, T.M. (1982), 'The real bills doctrine', Federal Reserve Bank of Richmond *Economic Review*, **68**, pp. 3–13; as reprinted in Humphrey (1986), pp. 80–90.

Humphrey, T.M. (1989), 'Lender of last resort: the concept in history', Federal Reserve Bank of Richmond *Economic Review*, **75**, pp. 8–16.

Kaldor, N. (1982), *The Scourge of Monetarism*, New York: Oxford University Press.

Kaldor, N. (1983), 'Keynesian economics after fifty years', in D. Worswick and J. Trevithick (eds), *Keynes and the Modern World*, Cambridge: Cambridge University Press, pp. 1–28.

Kaldor, N., and Trevithick, J. (1981), 'A Keynesian perspective on money', *Lloyds Bank Review*, **139**, pp. 1–19.

Keynes, J.M. (1936), *The General Theory of Employment, Interest and Money*, London: Macmillan.

Laidler, D. (1987), 'Bullionist controversy', in J. Eatwell, M. Milgate, and P. Newman (eds), *The New Palgrave*, vol. 1, pp. 289–94.

Mints, L. (1945), *A History of Banking Theory*, Chicago: University of Chicago Press.

Morgan, E.V. (1970), 'The Radcliffe report in the tradition of British official monetary documents', in D.R. Croome and H.G. Johnson (eds), *Money in Britain 1959–1969*, London: Oxford University Press, pp. 3–21.

Nurkse, R. (1946), *The Course and Control of Inflation: A Review of Monetary Experience in Europe After World War I*, Geneva: League of Nations.

O'Brien, D.P. (1975), *The Classical Economists*, London: Oxford University Press.

Robbins, L. (1958), *Robert Torrens and the Evolution of Classical Economics*, London: Macmillan.

Schumpeter, J. (1954), *History of Economic Analysis*, New York: Oxford University Press.

Schwartz, A. (1987), 'Banking school, currency school, free banking school', in J. Eatwell, M. Milgate, and P. Newman (eds) *The New Palgrave*, vol. 1, pp. 182–5.

Stigler, S. (1980), 'Stigler's law of eponymy', *Transactions of the New York Academy of Sciences*, Series II, **39**, pp. 147–58.

Thirlwall, A.P. (1988), *Nicholas Kaldor*, New York: New York University Press.

Thornton, H. (1802), *An Enquiry Into the Nature and Effects of the Paper Credit of Great Britain* (reprint 1939), London: George Allen and Unwin.

Viner, J. (1937), *Studies in the Theory of International Trade*, New York: Harper.

8 Commercial therapeutics and the banking profession in early Victorian England

Timothy L. Alborn[1]

Introduction

Since before the time of Adam Smith and the physiocrats, economists have compared the human body with the body politic to help them prescribe the proper relationship between economic theory and policy. By this means Smith countered the physiocratic notion that 'the political body ... would thrive and prosper only under a certain precise regimen', arguing that in such a body, as in the human frame, 'the wisdom of nature has fortunately made ample provision for remedying many of the bad effects of the folly and injustice of man'.[2] As is well known, Smith's appeal to natural law provided nineteenth-century capitalists with strong rhetorical weapons in their efforts to resist legislative interference. It also proved useful to the Victorian medical profession, who treated the human body at the source of his analogy, and who turned to the 'wisdom of nature' to preserve their authority from the threat of government bureaucrats and unlicensed practitioners. These parallel responses to competing therapeutic strategies can be attributed to the similar social standing and aspirations of the commercial and medical professions in Victorian England, and also to the availability of a powerful analogy linking the wealth and health of nations.

Throughout the nineteenth century the English people suffered from periodic crises that affected both their physical and economic well-being. Epidemic outbreaks of cholera and malaria, and disastrous financial events like the panic of 1847 and the failure of Overend, Gurney in 1866, proved stern antidotes to Victorian optimism. Controversies over different therapeutic approaches reached their peak at such times, attracting unwelcome attention to the professions who were responsible for keeping things running smoothly. As the statistician James Lawson observed after the 1847 crisis, 'Commercial panics are diseases to which the body politic is subject – not chronic diseases, but epidemics', providing 'one of the powerful means of drawing attention to political economy, just as human ailments called medicine into existence'.[3] Many economists tried to divert that attention onto bankers, whom they blamed for encouraging the overtrading that normally preceded monetary panics. In the most significant of these efforts, Sir Robert Peel and the 'Currency School' of economists accused country and joint-stock bankers of issuing more bank notes than the economy required, and responded by passing legislation that limited each bank's monthly circulation to a fixed sum above the amount of gold bullion in the bank of England. Peel's critics, loosely composing what has since been called the 'Banking School', criticized Parliament and political economists for sailing an untried theory in the face of years of practical commercial experience.[4]

The bankers' response to the Currency School exhibited striking rhetorical and methodological analogies to the early Victorian medical profession's approach to therapeutics. Rhetorically, commercial writers could not resist the temptation to compare Peel's prescriptions to those of a quack who promised more from his cure than it could possibly deliver. This treatment of Peel dated back two decades before the Bank Charter Act, when Sir Walter Scott attacked his attempted extension of banking legislation to Scotland in *Letters from Malachi Malagrowther* (1826). Scott compared Peel to an acquaintance who forced all his dinner guests to take patent medicine after eating, a telling simile that resurfaced whenever legislation threatened bankers' autonomy.[5] Even though the analogy between Peel and a medical quack was more entertaining than precise, it reflected deep-seated similarities between the selection of therapies by bankers and doctors. In contrast to the speculative promises of legislators or quack physicians, both professions stressed the curative powers of personal supervision based on individual experience.

This common response to competing therapies spilled over into attitudes about how to connect therapeutic work to contemporary medical and economic science. Through their practical eyes, the medical and banking professions viewed the theoretical foundations of anatomical theory and Ricardian economics as irrelevant, and potentially threatening, to their concerns. Whether writing about human anatomy or the economy, they argued, most self-acclaimed experts mused about cause and effect with little firsthand experience to support their conclusions. Doctors and bankers tried to keep such writers in check by developing alternative sciences designed to highlight the salient points of their respective professional agendas. Each group relied heavily on the emerging discipline of statistics to achieve this end, both for its capacity to locate empirical loopholes in competing theories and for its reigning popularity in early Victorian England as a prime example of truly Baconian science.[6] Their Baconian appeal to statistics allowed them to dispute received opinions as unscientific without having to offer coherent theories of their own. If, as they argued, all theories emerged out of statistical evidence, only the patient collection and arrangement of facts at the bedside and the bank counter would provide the requisite means for some day reaching scientific truth. While waiting for that day to arrive and urging the public to do the same, they worked on securing professional authority at their newly-defined loci of scientific investigation.

By the end of the nineteenth century, however, it became increasingly difficult for doctors and bankers to cloak claims of professional authority in the garb of Baconian statistical science. Bacteriology and neoclassical economics had emerged as strong sciences in their own right, suggesting tempting applications to medical and commercial therapeutics. Also, changing professional and economic conditions were leading doctors and bankers to re-evaluate their previous position on the proper relationship between theory and practice. Although germ theory and marginalism presented serious cognitive and institutional problems in application, they both eventually succeeded in becoming permanent fixtures, respectively, in the medical and banking communities. The remainder of the chapter will survey the professional development and corresponding therapeutics in each of these communities in early Victorian England, then conclude with a view of the therapeutic transition that commenced at the end of the nineteenth century.

The medical profession
The medical profession in early Victorian England has been described as 'a tangle of conflicting rights and powers'. At the beginning of the nineteenth century this tangle was broadly divided into three groups, consisting of physicians, surgeons and general practitioners. The first two enjoyed relatively high social status, control over medical education and prestigious locations in hospitals, all coming more from inherited social connections than from medical skill. General practitioners, conversely, while comprising the vast majority of doctors, were held back from status by the historically trade-oriented nature of their work, and unable to improve their position through traditional channels. To achieve professional recognition they tried to redefine the structure of British medicine, in organs and societies – such as the *Lancet* and the British Medical Association – that have since come to represent modern medical orthodoxy. The reformers tried to convince fellow practitioners as well as the lay public to support a medical education system that valued merit over gentility and public service over entrepreneurship.[7]

An active ingredient in the general practitioners' reform efforts was their appeal to a revised version of medical science, following the example of statistics and pathology then practised in Paris. After the French Revolution, the reorganised Paris hospital claimed international attention as a centre for clinical science, contrasting sharply with the status and function of English hospitals.[8] In England, as one reformer wrote in 1843, existing medical leaders were 'denizens of an aristocratic squire – acquaintances of the noble – agreeable fellows in society ... bustling men of business; any thing, in short, but those patronized humble beings – *men of science*'.[9] The reformer defined science, in this instance, more by its location (that is, the hospital rather than the study) than by its potential practical application – not a surprising situation

during the first half of the century, when competition among English practitioners was based more on social factors than on therapeutic skill. Even most
reformers, who embraced the Paris school for its promise of intellectual
prestige and professional reorganisation, stopped short of claiming that their
scientific brethren across the Channel could teach them much about healing.[10]

To observe such a link between medical science and practice in the early
Victorian period one must turn to America, where the social position of doctors
was more closely tied to their perceived medical skill. There, medical reformers
turned to the French school as a way of disputing the value of competing
therapies such as homeopathy and bleeding. They used clinical statistics to
compare mortality rates of patients in hospitals where different therapies were
used with those of 'the unwary and the sceptical, who neglect to resort to
remedies', to demonstrate that most medical interventions were ineffective,
and some even damaging, for the patient's recovery. Against such 'ill-judged
activity of others', the reformer Jacob Bigelow urged doctors to observe, and
follow, the higher dictates of nature: 'the physician is but the minister and
servant of nature', he reminded his audience; 'in [many] cases ... we can do
little more than follow in the train of disease and endeavor to aid nature in her
salutary intentions, or to remove obstacles out of her path.'[11]

As the nineteenth century lurched past its epidemic-ridden midpoint, concerns about public health led to an increased awareness of therapeutics on both
sides of the Atlantic. Partly due to their ineffectiveness during the cholera years
of 1848 and 1853, medical reformers in England found themselves under fire
from new directions, despite the fact that their professionalizing efforts were
starting to bear fruit. Government sanitary reformers and peddlers of patent
medicine, from opposite ends of the social spectrum, openly disputed the
medical profession's ability to resolve England's crisis in public health. The
most damaging attack came from the central government, personified by the
sanitary reformer Edwin Chadwick and his General Board of Health. At a time
when doctors were trying to attain government certification and civil service
positions, Chadwick excluded them from the Board on the logic that public
health was chiefly an 'application of the science of engineering, of which
medical men know nothing'. Through a combination of fortunate circumstance, professional strength and a successful rhetorical appeal to 'scientific
medicine', the doctors succeeded in blunting the effects of this snub. The
fortunate circumstance was Chadwick's replacement as President of the Board
by Sir Benjamin Hall, who harboured less animus toward doctors than had his
predecessor. Medical men took advantage of Hall's appointment by pressing
upon Parliament the need for cholera to be investigated, in the words of one
Lancet correspondent, by 'men of high *scientific* attainments' in order to 'discover the most *scientific* methods of controlling the disease'. Hall obliged by
appointing a Medical Council in 1855, which ultimately evolved into what has

been called a 'virtual monopoly' by doctors in certain areas of public health administration.[12]

While civil servants like Chadwick challenged medical therapeutics from above, quack doctors tried to do the same from below. Their chief threat lay not so much in stealing the doctors' limelight as in dragging them back down to a pre-reform level. By offering patent medicines and secret cures directly to the public, heterodox physicians attempted to detour the meritocratic hurdles that medical reformers had set in the way of professional advancement. By profusely advertising those cures and charging for them by the bottle, they threatened a return to the days when doctors were perceived as 'bustling men of business'. Although quackery continued to be a thorn in the side of the medical profession throughout the nineteenth century, however, its effects could be mitigated through such internal measures as strict licensing and ostracism. As the profession grew in strength, these disciplinary remedies grew in potency.[13]

The banking profession

Many of the concerns that motivated general practitioners to respond with a professional alternative to competing therapies closely resembled the concerns of the emerging banking profession in Victorian England. The main participants in the move toward professional standards among bankers were managers of joint-stock banks, who occupied the same position in society as general practitioners and shared their aspirations for social elevation through meritocratic advancement.

Their main opponents within the profession also paralleled the situation in medicine. On one side, the 'charmed circle' of London private bankers, who used their individual fortunes as capital and their social position as guarantees for their liability, threatened joint-stock bankers in the same way that surgeons threatened general practitioners. On the other, private provincial banks threatened to bring joint-stock managers down to the level of a trade mentality that treated deposits as acceptable fodder for mercantile speculation and that lent credibility to claims that bankers were to blame for commercial crises. The emerging banking profession tried to avert such claims by promising the security of shareholder liability and the additional advantage of uniformly conservative administrative principles.[14]

As with doctors, the joint-stock bankers' efforts to achieve professional esteem included a redefinition of science to suit their practical position. Writers like J.W. Gilbart – the general manager of London's first and most successful joint-stock bank and a leading spokesman for the profession – promoted banking as a central branch of political economy by attempting to dethrone orthodox Ricardian theory. Gilbart measured the soundness of a system of political economy by its proven ability to produce practical results, rather than by its logical coherence, comparing it most closely to medical science, in which '[t]he surest proof of good treatment is the recovery of the patient'. Such results, in the science of banking, could be traced through statistics providing *post hoc* proofs of proper practice, but limiting the explanation of events to an implicit equation between economic growth and sound bank administration. Gilbart's definition of economic science corresponded to his professional definition of bankers, whom he described as 'public conservators of the commercial virtues' and whose primary job was to maintain the moral and social conditions in which successful banking could take place.[15]

Applied to commercial therapeutics, this version of economics conveniently prescribed a strong banking profession, free from legislative interference, as the only sure prevention of economic ills. Just as Gilbart interpreted medicine in the American sense of 'judging by results', he connected science to practice along the lines of the 'therapeutic skepticism' popular across the ocean. The moral of his statistical work, in fact, almost duplicated Jacob Bigelow's prescription for doctors to 'aid nature in her salutary intentions, or to remove obstacles out of her path' – a medical appeal that, when translated into economics, emerged as an unbending defence of *laissez faire*. Thus he presented his 'laws of the currency', which charted regionally specific regularities in monthly note circulation, as proof that 'the circulation must fluctuate according to the demands of trade and agriculture'.[16] The banker, in this situation, could offer moral guidance only in cases where 'unnatural' occurrences such as speculative manias threatened to interfere with the natural harmony of interests underlying the system. His only additional recourse was the type of professional reform then current among joint-stock bankers, consisting in the exposure and removal of the 'obstacles' of unenlightened banking habits among the English and unfair privileges of the Bank of England and private London bankers.

The Bank Charter Act represented a common focal point for these obstacles to free banking and hence appeared to justify the vociferous response launched by Gilbart and other members of the 'Banking School'. By appealing directly to public suspicion of joint-stock bankers and by boasting the support of eminent London private bankers like Lord Overstone and George Warde Norman, the Currency School posed a threat to Gilbart's commercial therapeutics equal to that posed by Chadwick's sanitary engineers to the medical community.[17] Like doctors, bankers were offended by their exclusion: as the editor of the *Bankers' Magazine* decried in 1844, 'Sir Robert Peel might have made his measure far more perfect and more acceptable to the commercial community, had he consulted practical Bankers previous to laying his plans before Parliament'. At mid-century, however, they were much less organized than their peers in the medical profession and could not hope for the sort of lobbying effort that doctors used to attain status in the civil service. Rather they lashed out at

Peel in the same language that doctors reserved for quacks – ridiculing the 'ready fluency of Sir Robert Peel' and the 'incoherent verbosity' of his economic experts – but lacked the professional authority to remove him from the public spotlight.[18]

Fortunately for the bankers' professional aspirations, if not for their financial success, the Bank Charter Act did not prove to be the panacea for economic ills that its constructors had predicted. While the currency principle did exercise some influence on the actual volume of notes issued, it fared less well as a mechanical failsafe against bank failure. The commercial crises of 1847, 1857 and 1866, all of which were alleviated only by suspending the Act, gave bankers the advantage of hindsight in their criticisms of the Currency School, an advantage further increased by Gilbart's practical reworking of economics along statistical lines. Gilbart returned to the rhetorical power of his allegedly natural laws of the currency after the crisis of 1847, to argue that his view of the economy was more 'scientific' and therefore more neutral. In 1854 he informed the London Statistical Society that 'questions relating to the currency are no longer connected with party politics, but are now regarded as presenting topics for scientific investigation; and we believe that by no science can they be more clearly and successfully investigated than by the science of statistics'. Scientific investigation, in this case, snugly fit Gilbart's professional aspirations by showing that the 'caprice of the bankers', if truly controlled by Peel's Act, could not have been the true cause of the recent economic crisis; and by attributing much more caprice to Peel's uniform application of his principles to an economy that Gilbart had statistically shown to exhibit regionally specific regularities.[19]

Since in Gilbart's empirical economics the proof of a principle could be determined by its results, the suspension of the Bank Charter Act in 1847 led him to conclude that the currency principle 'could not bear . . . the test of experiment' and left him optimistic that his 'antagonist principle' of competing issues and multiple bank reserves would take its place. But merely demonstrating that Peel's 'certain and precise regimen' was an ineffective therapy for England's economic woes did not automatically ensure that the 'natural wisdom' of free trade would succeed it. Although joint-stock banks did indeed flourish in the second half of the nineteenth century, the Bank of England also grew in size as the nation's main cash reserve, magnifying its directors' responsibility. In addition, even where free trade did prevail in banking, it did not always prove as wise as Gilbart had anticipated. The extension of limited liability to banks in 1857, for instance, swamped the money market with bankers who paid little heed to professional prescriptions of moral supervision and cautious calculation. And although Gilbart's heirs in the banking profession tried to quell this threat by blacklisting such firms, their efforts at standardization of practice did not match the success that their medical counterparts enjoyed in ostracizing quacks.[20] Victorian bill brokers and discount houses did not simply disappear, as did many contemporary heterodox physicians; and when one did disappear – Overend, Gurney being the stellar instance – the shock to the commercial system threatened to bring all banks, good and bad, down with it.

Therapeutic transitions

The discovery of germ theory in the 1880s introduced a new form of science into the medical community, promising techniques of intervention radical enough to jar many doctors into rethinking their traditional approach to therapeutics. With this rethinking came a number of difficult choices about how best to integrate bacteriological discovery into clinical practice. In one sense, germ theory offered doctors a much more impressive version of the 'medical science' they had been trying to wed to the profession for years. But this was a new sort of science, suggesting direct therapeutic applications in addition to the usual rhetorical advantages. Although doctors recognized the professional esteem accompanying a connection with 'pure science', many balked at the thought of sacrificing their traditional bedside therapeutics, or at least a significant part of it, to scientists in the bacteriological laboratory. To add to their ambivalence, such institutional changes were taking place at a period when the full consequences of germ theory were not fully understood by scientists, let alone doctors. A combination of such factors led many late-nineteenth century practitioners to scoff at the 'bacteriomania' that had infected so many of their peers, a reaction that reverberated well into the next century.[21]

As bacteriologists made gradual inroads into the medical community, neoclassical economists attempted to do the same in the business world. Led by the example of Alfred Marshall's *Industry and Trade* (1887), workers in the marginalist paradigm tried to apply mathematical economics to the practical world of banking and finance. A prime example of such an effort was Francis Edgeworth's 'Mathematical Theory of Banking', read before the British Association in 1886, in which he calculated the proper margin at which the Bank of England could maintain a reserve large enough to provide ample security in times of crisis without sacrificing the highest possible dividend for its shareholders. As in the medical community, but for different reasons, bankers' responses to such efforts were mixed. Part of the problem was that the neoclassical claim of practical application was much weaker than the parallel claim in bacteriology: even Edgeworth was forced to admit that his theoretical observations were 'at an immense height of abstraction above the affairs of earth' and he did not 'pretend to base any practical recommendations upon the theory'.[22] Yet bankers still listened to Edgeworth, for reasons having more to do with changing commercial and professional conditions than with the actual content of neoclassical economics.

By the close of the century, bankers had abandoned Gilbart's idealistic scenario of a multi-reserve system of competing issues in favour of a more realistic view of the economy and its proper therapeutics. The leading advocate of this approach was Walter Bagehot, who waxed nostalgic for the 'natural' system of many banks of issue but firmly declared that the habits of Englishmen could not be stirred from their unreasoning loyalty to the Bank of England. He thus concluded *Lombard Street* with the lament that 'there is nothing for it but to make the best of our banking system, and to work it in the best way that it is capable of. We can only use palliatives, and the point is to get the best palliatives we can'. His chief palliative was to pressure the Bank of England into maintaining a reserve large enough to meet its responsibility as England's central bank of deposit. Economists offered promising means of raising the political support needed to enact stricter Bank regulation and although Bagehot himself would have doubted Edgeworth's pretentions to predictive certainty,[23] later bankers were more willing to listen. One such banker was Robert Palgrave, a stout supporter of Bagehot's palliatives and active liaison with neoclassical economists.[24] By settling on Bank of England policy as a focal point for commercial therapeutics, bankers and economists finally found a way to transfer their suspicions of each other to a third party and finally established a loose set of rules for arbitrating between economic theory and practice.

Today, the ethos of personal care that marked the nineteenth-century therapeutics of medical reformers has by and large given way to an ethos of laboratory testing. The medical technician has come to marginalize the general practictioner, in the sense that while people still turn to their family doctor when they get sick, that doctor turns to a specialist when any serious problems arise. In the process, medical science has undergone a social and economic, as well as technical, transformation in meaning; the doctor today appeals to science less as an aid for professional status or as a foil against competing therapies (although both of these appeals remain) and more as a separate institutionalized entity with a vast stock of therapeutic resources. A similar, though less striking, transition has taken place in the world of banking. Most large banks today include in their organization an economics department which is kept institutionally separate from the side of the office which caters to the depositor or loan applicant. In each case, the choice of therapeutics, and the corresponding relations between science and practice, have undergone changes that have seriously affected the versions of medicine and commerce passed down to the present.

Notes

1. The author wishes to thank N.B. de Marchi for his helpful comments on a draft of this chapter.
2. Adam Smith, (1776, p. 638).
3. James Lawson, (1848, pp. 415–20); 415q. In his Gilbart Lectures on Banking, the mercantile lawyer Leone Levi called a panic 'the Asiatic cholera of the commercial world, epidemic, most contagious, and fatal'; *Bankers' Magazine*, supplement, 35(1875, p. 94).
4. On the more general features of the Currency School/ Banking School debate see F.W. Fetter, (1965); D.P. O'Brien, (1971, i, pp. 70–144) and T.E. Gregory, (1928). Lawrence H. White, (1984), challenges the arbitrary term 'banking school', and clarifies important differences separating, for instance, Tooke and J.W. Gilbart on the issue of Bank of England responsibility. On the contemporary criticism that political economists made bad legislators because they did not appreciate economic reality, see the all too brief section in N.B. de Marchi (1974, pp. 124–5).
5. Walter Scott, (1826, pp. 5–6); the pamphleteer James Taylor, for instance, (1845, p. 3), warned: 'Beware of Peel's Nostrums. His words are softer than butter, but his prescriptions are gall and wormwood.'
6. On the status of statistical science in England see Theodore M. Porter, (1986), and Lawrence Goldman, (1983, pp. 587–616).
7. M. Jeanne Peterson, (1978, p. 5q).
8. See Erwin H. Ackerknecht, (1967). Louis was famous for applying Quetelet's 'numerical method' to pathology.
9. *Medical Times*, 14(1846, p. 220); cited in John Harley Warner, (forthcoming).
10. Warner (forthcoming).
11. Jacob Bigelow, (1836); On theory and practice in American science see Warner, (1985, pp. 213–31), and Charles E. Rosenberg, (1979, pp. 3–25).
12. Steven J. Novak, (1973, pp. 440–62; quotations by Chadwick from the *Lancet* are reprinted by Novak on pp. 447–9); Margaret Pelling, (1978). Doctors whom Chadwick did support, such as William Farr and Thomas Southwood-Smith, were roundly condemned by most general practitioners.
13. Peterson (1978, pp. 256–9).
14. Although business historians have written much on Scottish banking, modern accounts of the English counterpart are scarce. Walter Bagehot (1874, ix, pp. 45–233) remains a highly readable introduction; see also S. Evelyn Thomas, (1934, vol. i).
15. Gilbart, (1841, p. 33); (1851a, p. 147); (1851b, p. 8).
16. Gilbart, (1844, p. 459). Gilbart's statistical findings were presented the most completely from 1852 through 1856 in the *Statistical Journal*.
17. In fact, it was Peel who set Chadwick's General Board of Health in motion by appointing a Royal Commission on the Health of Towns in 1844, the same year he passed the Bank Charter Act.
18. John Dalton in *Bankers' Magazine*, 7(1847, p. 254); also *Bankers' Magazine*, 6 (1846, pp. 134, 81).
19. Gilbart, (1854, p. 289); (1856, p. 155). Gilbart's appeal to natural law to argue that the 'caprice of bankers' was not responsible for commercial crisis opened the way for some extreme *laissez faire* writers to counter that bankers could not have it both ways: either they were responsible for crisis, or not responsible for growth. The commercial writer John Francis, for instance, who joined Gilbart in criticizing the Currency School for interfering with the natural laws of the currency, praised times of economic crisis for directly producing growth by weeding out the good companies from the bad, and argued that bankers were powerless to prevent such 'inscrutible decree[s] of Providence'. Gilbart responded by comparing Francis's solution to the barbarous medical therapies practised before the age of reform: 'If we never indulged in excess, we should have no need of bleeding and blistering; therefore, as with the physical so with the commercial body, prudence and regularity [are] the only means of avoiding the necessity' of crisis. See Francis (1852, pp. 557–64; including Gilbart's reply).

20. Gilbart (1851b, pp. 74–5); (1859, p. 414). On the rise of bill brokers and discount houses at the fringes of the Victorian money market, see P.L. Cottrell, (1985).
21. See Russell C. Maulitz (1979, pp. 91–107); and Barbara Gutman Rosenkrantz, (1985).
22. Edgeworth, (1888, pp. 113–27).
23. Bagehot, (1874, pp. 80–1, 215). On p. 210 of *Lombard Street*, as well as many other places in his economic writings, Bagehot revealed his suspicion of economists' mathematical pretensions: 'nothing but experience can tell us what amount of "reserve" will create a diffused confidence; on such a subject there is no way of arriving at a just conclusion except by incessantly watching the public mind, and seeing at each juncture how it is affected'.
24. Palgrave expressed his support of Bagehot's principles (1874, pp. 92–108); for his alliance with the neo-classicals, see the *Dictionary of Political Economy*, edited by Palgrave.

References

Ackerknecht, E.H. (1967), *Medicine at the Paris Hospital, 1794–1848*, Baltimore and London: Johns Hopkins University Press.

Bagehot, W. (1874), *Lombard Street*, repr. (1978), in *Collected Works*, London: The Economist.

Bigelow, J. (1836), 'On Self-limited Diseases', repr. in G.H. Brieger (ed.), (1972), *Medical America in the Nineteenth Century*, Baltimore: Johns Hopkins University Press, pp. 96–106, 106q.

Cottrell, P.L. (1985), *Investment Banking in England 1856–1881: a Case Study of the International Financial Society*, New York: Garland.

Edgeworth, F.Y. (1888), 'The Mathematical Theory of Banking', *Statistical Journal*, **51**.

Fetter, F.W. (1965), *Development of the British Monetary Orthodoxy 1797–1875*, Cambridge MA: Harvard University Press.

Francis, J. (1852), 'Commercial Crises', *Bankers' Magazine*, **12**.

Gilbart, J.W. (1841), *Currency and Banking*, London: H. Hooper.

Gilbart, J.W. (1844), 'The Laws of Currency', repr. in (1859), *The Logic of Banking: a Familiar Exposition of the Principles of Reasoning, and their Application to the Art and Science of Banking*, London: Longman, Brown, Green, Longmans and Roberts.

Gilbart, J.W. (1851a), *Logic for the Millions*, 5th. ed. (1857), London: Longman, Brown, Green and Longmans.

Gilbart, J.W. (1851b), *Practical Treatise of Banking*, 5th. ed., London and New York: Longman, Brown, Green and Longmans.

Gilbart, J.W. (1854), 'The Laws of Currency, as Exemplified in the Circulation of Country Bank Notes in England', *Statistical Journal*, **17**.

Gilbart, J.W. (1856), 'The Laws of Currency in Scotland', *Statistical Journal*, **19**.

Goldman, L. (1983), 'The Origins of British "Social Science": Political Economy, Natural Science and Statistics, 1830–1835', *Historical Journal*, **26**.

Gregory, T.E. (1928), 'Introduction', in T. Tooke and W. Newmarch, *A History of Prices*, New York: Adelphi.

Lawson, J. (1848), 'The Cause of Commercial Panics', (Dublin Statistical Society Paper), repr. *Bankers' Magazine*, **8**.

de Marchi, N.B. (1974), 'The Success of Mill's *Principles*', *History of Political Economy*, **6**.

Maulitz, R.C. (1979), '"Physician versus Bacteriologist": the Ideology of Science in Clinical Medicine', in M.J. Vogel and C. Rosenberg (eds), *The Therapeutic Revolution: Essays in the Social History of American Medicine*, Philadelphia: University of Pennsylvania Press.

Novak, S.J. (1973), 'Professionalism and Bureaucracy: English Doctors and the Victorian Public Health Administration', *Journal of Social History*, **6**.

O'Brien, D.P. (1971), 'Introduction', *The Correspondence of Lord Overstone*, Cambridge: Cambridge University Press.

Palgrave, R.H.I. (1874), 'Banking', *Fornightly Review*, **21**.

Palgrave, R.H.I. (ed.), (1894–99), *Dictionary of Political Economy*, 3 vols, London: Macmillan.

Pelling, M. (1978), *Cholera, Fever and English Medicine 1825–1865*, Oxford: Oxford University Press.

Peterson, M.J. (1978), *The Medical Profession in Mid-Victorian London*, Berkeley: University of California Press.

Porter, T.M. (1986), *The Rise of Statistical Thinking in England, 1815–1900*, Princeton: Princeton University Press.

Rosenberg, C.E. (1979), 'The Therapeutic Revolution: Medicine, Meaning and Social Change in Nineteenth-Century America', in M.J. Vogel and C. Rosenberg (eds), *The Therapeutic Revolution: Essays in the Social History of American Medicine*, Philadelphia: University of Pennsylvania Press.

Rosenkrantz, B.G. (1985), 'The Search for Professional Order in 19th-Century American Medicine', in J. Leavitt and R. Numbers (eds), *Sickness and Health in America*, 2nd edn, Madison: University of Wisconsin Press.

Scott, W. (1826), *Letters from Malachi Malagrowther, Esq. on the Proposed Change of Currency*, 3rd edn, 1844, Edinburgh: William Blackwood.

Smith, A. (1776), *Wealth of Nations*, reprinted 1937, New York: Modern Library.

Taylor, J. (1845), *John Bull's Letter to Malachi Malagrowther, Esquire, of North Britain, on the Premier's Currency*, London: Aylott and Jones.

Thomas, S.E. (1934), *The Rise and Growth of Joint Stock Banking*, London: Sir I. Pitman and Sons.

Warner, J.H. (1985), 'The Selective Transport of Medical Knowledge: Antebellum American Physicians and Parisian Medical Therapeutics', in *Bulletin of the History of Medicine*, **59**.

Warner, J.H. (forthcoming), 'The Idea of Science in English Medicine: the "Decline of Science" and the Rhetoric of Reform 1815–1845', in R. French and A. Wear (eds), *The Birth of Modern British Medicine, 1760–1840*.

White, L.H. (1984), *Free Banking in Britain*, Cambridge: Cambridge University Press.

PART IV

TOPICS IN THE ECONOMICS OF MARXISM

9   Why *Das Kapital* remained unfinished

Zoltan Kenessey[1]

Introduction

The present turmoil and realignments in the economies of the Soviet Union, Hungary, Poland and other countries in Eastern Europe provide an intriguing backdrop to the topic of this chapter. If one assumes that the economic problems of these countries are, at least in part, related to their past claims regarding Marxist economic postulates, then the unfinished nature of *Das Kapital* raises the puzzling question: have the planners and economic policy makers in those countries relied on an incomplete framework, which its originator could not finish?

Moreover, if this is correct, and Marx recognized the impossible nature of his task (at least under the limitations of his times), have his contemporaries and followers (starting with Engels) failed to understand his intellectual dilemma, and done a disservice to him and to mankind by patching together his manuscripts and fragments for the second and third volumes of *Das Kapital*? In short, could we assume that Marx did not finish *Das Kapital* because he could not and would not complete it without the resolution of certain important matters, for which no solution existed in his time (and probably not even today)?

Interesting conjectures of this sort cannot be proved or disproved, certainly not beyond reasonable doubt. Even less can they address whether or not Marx's followers in China, Russia, Hungary or Poland have indeed implemented economic measures in line with his thoughts. It was shown long ago by Kolakowski that arguments of this sort are usually ideologically 'loaded'.[2]

This chapter considers the unfinished character of *Das Kapital* solely from the viewpoint of the history of economic thought. Without attempting to answer the broader questions of significance of the matter, it merely puts the undisputed facts regarding the incomplete manuscripts of *Das Kapital* (edited and issued after Marx's death as Volumes II and III) into perspectives provided by the correspondence of Marx and some other materials. These indicate Marx's desire to develop an economic theory of the business cycle in terms of mathematical laws based on statistical observations for interest rates and other economic variables.

Among the materials and manuscripts left behind by Marx are certain notebooks which corroborate Marx's interest in collecting statistical material for at least two of the major cyclical downturns in his time. These and other manifestations of his statistical interest, coupled with extensive studies of mathematics, strongly indicate that the intent suggested in the Marx correspondence was not casual. But the age of Marx was not yet ripe for macroeconometric model building (to use the jargon of our age), perhaps a major reason for leaving *Das Kapital* unfinished.

The letter of 31 May 1873

At the end of May 1873 Marx wrote a letter to Engels, which contains the following passage:

> ...I told here Moore a story, with which I have been struggling at length privately. He thinks, however, that the matter cannot be solved, or it is, because of the manifold and mostly still to be explored factors involved in it, pro tempore unsolvable. This is how the matter stands: You know the tables in which prices, discount-rate, etc. etc. are shown according to their movements during the year as up and down zig-zags. I have tried several times – for the analysis of the crises – to calculate these ups and downs as irregular curves, and I thought (I still believe that with adequately-sorted material it is possible) to determine mathematically the main laws of the crisis. Moore, as I said, considers the task at present unsolvable, and I have decided for the time being to give it up ... [3]

This letter first came to our attention in the late 1950s in Hungary. At that time in Eastern Europe, but particularly in the Soviet Union, the application of mathematical techniques in economics was considered a negative (Western) ideological influence. Hence Marx's interest in the subject was useful in the controversy about the proper direction of economic research in the Eastern European countries, and as an argument supporting the use of contemporary economic tools, such as input-output techniques and econometric modelling in a socialist setting. Over the decades many references were made to this letter by economists in various countries. For example in Japan a quotation from this Marx letter served as a justification for Koshimura's two-volume extension of the mathematical cycle theory of Marx. Koshimura, after quoting from the letter, suggested that 'Marx, however, could not realize his wish because of his illness. In my opinion fulfilling his intention will lay a corner-stone for the development of Marxian economics, because as Marx says, "a science does not truly bloom till it can utilize mathematics"'. [4]

Koshimura was certainly not the only commentator to attribute the unfinished state of the manuscripts of *Das Kapital* to Marx's illness. The New Palgrave also suggests that 'Bad health was probably the main reason why the final versions of vols II and III of Capital could not be finished'. [5] Also his political activities (such as the work with the International), the pressures to earn money beyond the funds available through Engels's support, and the Marx family's many tribulations are considered as other explanatory factors for the uncompleted state of *Das Kapital*. There is no doubt that throughout his stay in London (where he also died and was buried in Highgate Cemetery) Marx was beset by bouts of ill health, was subject to grave financial problems, and lost several children, among them his only son, Edgar.

The larger intellectual difficulties involved in Marx's comprehensive project, however, have not received appropriate attention. This chapter considers the proposition that such intellectual problems probably hampered the completion of Marx's *magnum opus* more profoundly than is generally realized. Marx was aware of various obstacles to his plan; he certainly knew Moore's doubts about it, and indicated that he intended at least 'temporarily' to give up his pursuit of this approach. We believe, however, that he never entirely abandoned his intentions.

The Amsterdam notebooks
Many of the manuscripts of Marx are housed in Amsterdam, in the archives of the International Institute of Social History. The archival materials document that Marx, especially during the times of economic downturns, maintained special notebooks in which he collected data on interest rates, bankruptcies, and so on. An article describing these documents in some detail was published in 1962, so here we only refer to their overall scope and general character.[6]

Notebooks marked B 82 and B 87 deal with the economic downturn of 1857. The designation of the first is 'Book of the crisis of 1857. London, 12 December 1857. (commenced)'; the second is titled 'The Book of the Commercial Crisis, January, 1858'. The notebooks contain 60 and 61 large size pages, respectively. The first book has materials from November, December, and January (mostly for December 1858) in the form of newspaper cuttings, tables compiled by Marx, items of news, references to data, and so on. The continuing second book covers materials from 30 December 1857 to 17 February 1858. Apparently Marx thought through the structure of the second book on the basis of his experience with the first, which was much less systematic. The system used in the second book, as designated by Marx in English (and shown according to his spelling) was the following:[7]

1. Moneymarket
1. Bank of England
2. Bullionmarket
    a) Aflux and Influx of Bullion
    b) Price and Movement of Silver
    c) Foreign Exchanges
3. Loan Market
4. Failures
5. Security Market

 a) Share Market
 b) Public Funds

II. Producemarket
1. Raw materials for textile fabrics
 a) Cotton
 b) Silk
 c) Wool
 d) Hemp and flax
2. Metals
3. Hides and leather
4. Mincinglane [8]
5. Cornmarket

III. Industrial Market

IV. Labourmarket

V. Miscellaneous

A similar notebook, marked B 105 in Amsterdam, contains materials compiled by Marx ten years later. This one is 86 pages long and it is designated 'History of Commerce, 1868'. This book contains only handwritten entries (no clippings from newspapers, etc.) – perhaps he could not afford to purchase the relevant papers and magazines and copied the necessary items into his notebook from library holdings. The sources indicated in the book are mostly the *Economist* and the *Money Market Review*.

Of particular interest are the notebook entries culled from the weekly reports of the Bank of England concerning the circulation of banknotes, the deposits in the Bank, movement of bullion, and the reserves of the Bank. There is also a table of the discount rate with data from 1845 to 1857. This may be the kind of table to which reference is made in the Marx letter of 31 May 1873. The table has several data entries for most years of the period, and for each date shows (*a*) the Bank of England's minimum discount rate, (*b*) the gold reserves, (*c*) the highest and lowest London broker discount rate for each of the years involved. The source of the table is not indicated; presumably it was cut out of the *Times* by Marx. Part of the note to the table, also contained in the cut-out, says: 'The respective periods of 1847 and 1857 are sufficiently marked to show the course of the panic at those particular dates.'

Other references pertain to the import of precious metals, to foreign payments, and to the situation of the credit markets. Particular attention was paid by Marx to reports on bankruptcies. He registered, for example, three bankruptcies for 8 December 1857, giving the serial numbers 8,9, and 10 to them and listing the name of each company, its field of activity ('Norwegian commerce', 'German commerce'), and the value involved ('170,000', '100,000'). Still other entries contain stock quotations, weekly data on railroad traffic (passengers and freight), prices of raw materials and products, the import of cotton, and so on. Some Mincing Lane entries are quite detailed by type of item, for example, coffee by places of origin, prices of sugar. A table dated 'January 6 (Wednesday)' [1858] contains data on the employment situation in Manchester and lists separately for cotton weavers, silk weavers, the machine industry, and so on, the number of workers generally employed (a total of 46 404), the number of workers currently fully employed (18 594), the number on shortened working time (19 077), and number of unemployed (8 733). The availability of such information, of course, attests to the early development of economic statistics in England, far ahead of other countries in 1857.

Other Amsterdam materials
According to the evidence of the excerpts marked B 106 in Amsterdam, Marx studied in detail the important source book of the time, Otto Hausner's *Vergleichende Statistik für Europa* (Comparative Statistics for Europe), issued in Hamburg in 1861. Marx's notebooks based on Hausner's book are filled with statistical tables and data series. Apparently Marx did not have a personal copy of this reference work, hence the need for the extensive excerpts.

The notes marked B 41 contain very early materials ('Notes from the *Economist* 1848'). These include data on cotton for the years 1843/44 through 1848, the annual exports of England between 1836 and 1848, and so on. In the excerpts marked B 102, other statistical tables are shown: for example the profits of the Bank of England between 1844 and 1866.

Data on countries other than England are much sparser among the notes archived in Amsterdam. In part, this may reflect the wider availability of statistics and other reports for England, and the fact that Marx lived in London; but some of the materials pertaining to other countries may have been lost, or are yet to be discovered. A letter from Marx to Engels, dated 18 December 1857 (a time at which Marx was preoccupied with following the economic crisis) makes explicit reference to three notebooks:

> ... I work quite intensively [*ganz kolossal*] mostly up to four o'clock in the morning. Namely the work is twofold: *1*. The elaboration of the outline of economics ... *2*. The present crisis ... [underlined by Marx.] I have laid out three large books – England, Germany, France. [The three country names are in English in the otherwise German text.] The story regarding America are to be found all in the Tribune.[9]

Another reference by Marx to materials pertaining to non-English economic circumstances is in a letter written to Engels one week later (dated 25 December 1857 – apparently Marx's preoccupation with the economic crisis was not stopped for Christmas Day): 'As our first task is now to see the French conditions clearly, I once again went through all my excerpts about French commerce, industry and crises ...'.[10]

References in non-archival sources

In contrast to the statistical materials mentioned, we were not able to locate notes or calculations regarding the mathematical explanation of the cycle. This may have been due to the limited time available for the search, or to the location of such materials elsewhere. On the other hand, over the decades these calculations may have been lost, or Marx may not have carried them out after all. The probability of the last eventuality does not seem to be very high. The letter of 31 May 1873 is rather unequivocal about the matter (indicating Marx's lengthy preoccupation with the problem, his several attempts regarding it, as well as his faith in its ultimate feasibility). Also, the approach in question is very much in line with Marx's general world view and inclination to establish economic and social theory as a science. It should be recalled that the Marxian edifice was always called 'scientific socialism' by later Marxists in contrast to the 'utopian socialism' which preceded it.

Moreover, Marx's interest in business cycles can be validated from non-archival sources as well. For example, Marx in his 'British Commerce and Finance' of 14 September 1858 stressed the following requirements in connection with the analysis of the cycle: 'In the attempts to demonstrate the laws, which govern the crises of the world market, not only their periodic character must be explained, but also the exact dates of these periodic returns'. In this analysis Marx also criticized the English Parliamentary reports of the times: '... they treat each new crisis as an isolated phenomenon appearing for the first time on the social horizon. ... If natural scientists carried out themselves in the same childish way, even the reappearance of a comet would surprise the world'.[11]

An even more colourful reference to Marx's scientific aspirations regarding business cycle analysis is in his letter to Engels of 13 November 1857:

> ... I have proven in a thorough article in the Tribune, now that the whole statement is before us, [the eight words in this clause between the two commas are in English in the otherwise German text] and even solely from the table of the discountrates [this word is also in English, as shown] from 1848 to 1854, that normally the crisis should have taken place two years earlier. Also the delays [word in English] can now be explained so rationally that Hegel himself, to his great satisfaction, would again find the 'idea' in the 'empirical dispersion of the finite interests of the world'.[12]

The references to rationality and to Hegel are unmistakable signs of Marx's belief in the applicability of scientific (hence rational and mathematical) approaches to the business cycle, and relate to his conviction that such an approach can be based on actual statistical observations for the economy.

Marx's attempts to show the regularities of the business cycle apparently always involved discussions of the movements in interest rates. It seems that this concatenation occurred for both theoretical and statistical reasons. The theoretical context is discussed on p. 126. Concerning the statistical reasons, both the availability of historical data on interest rates and Marx's access to frequent current observations on interest rates ought to be mentioned. In short: interest rates were a very important cyclical variable for Marx, and a series for which data were at hand (in an age of relative paucity of statistics). An interesting discussion of the interest rate and cyclical movements was printed in an article by Marx in the *New York Tribune*, 30 November 1857. Most likely this is the work referred to by Marx in his letter to Engels of 13 November 1857. It describes the action of the Bank of England in raising the rates in October and November of 1857 and compares the situation with the developments during the 1847 crisis, the downward movement of the rate through 1852, and the ensuing upturn of interest between 1852 and 1857. In his lengthy discussion of the matter Marx points to the relationship of interest rate movements and the periodic phases of modern commerce.

The third volume of *Das Kapital*

As mentioned earlier, in contrast to Volume I of *Das Kapital*, which was published by Marx in 1867, the manuscripts of the second and third volumes were left behind in an incomplete state at the time of his death in 1883. Indeed Engels was astonished by the degree of incompleteness of the materials (especially for the third volume). He was faced with a monumental task of editing and completing the manuscripts. As a result of his efforts Volume II was published relatively soon, in 1885, but Volume III (the one of particular interest to us) appeared only in 1894.

From the viewpoint of the analysis of the business cycle, the third volume of *Das Kapital* is the crucial one. The general outline of Marx's project called for a treatment of the more abstract basic concepts of his economics (such as use value, exchange value, and surplus value) first, and the fleshing out of the actual reproduction cycle later. The implementation of this approach led later critics to examine the differences between the Marxian treatment of certain issues (especially the rate of profit) in the more abstract text of the first volume and in the more elaborate and concrete presentation in the third volume. The matter of surplus value as explained in the first volume and the transformation of it, through the producer price and average rate of profit as described in the third volume, is probably the most celebrated issue of this kind.

In 1858 Marx indicated to Engels that within the 'six books' of *Das Kapital*, he envisaged the interconnected discussion of international commerce and world markets in the last two parts.[13] This intent was in line with the general approach accepted by Marx for his project: first a more abstract and restricted treatment of the matters was provided, but in later expositions he planned a relaxation of certain initial restrictions. Thus in respect of foreign trade Marx first assumed the existence of a completely closed economy and carried out his analysis without regard to the complications of international ramifications, but intended to relax this abstraction, as the 1858 reference shows, in the concluding parts of *Das Kapital*.

It seems likely that he envisaged more elaborate references to the business cycle in the later books as well. It can be supposed that the results of his statistical investigations and studies of the major economies of his age would have influenced this part. We have already mentioned Marx's interest in the data of England, France and Germany in the context of his Amsterdam notebooks. There are many indications of similar efforts elsewhere and for other countries. For example, the letter from Friedrich Engels to Sorge of 29 June 1883 contains the following reference to Marx's statistical preoccupations: 'Had not been there a huge American and Russian material (the Russian statistics alone consisted of more than two cubic meter of books), the Second Volume [of *Das Kapital*] would have been printed long ago. These detailed studies delayed him for years'.[14]

Marx's appreciation of statistical materials, especially the ones pertaining to England, was also clearly expressed in the warm acknowledgements of these sources in his Introduction to the first volume of *Das Kapital* in 1867.[15] Lenin said that while writing his *magnum opus* Marx worked through a 'Mont Blanc of facts'. More importantly, Engels indicated in the Preface to the third edition of *Das Kapital*, some 15 years after the first edition appeared, that 'Marx had it in mind to undertake a thorough revision of the present volume, to clarify many of the theoretical discussions, to add new matter, to supplement the historical and statistical material by bringing it up to date'.[16]

The interest rate and the cycle

As already mentioned, Marx's work on business cycle analysis always involved the study of interest rate movements. The availability of historical and current data on interest rates facilitated this approach. However, a more fundamental reason was Marx's attention to interest rates on theoretical grounds. Thus it is not surprising that the analysis of interest rates is a major feature of the third volume of *Das Kapital*. About 250 pages out of a total of about 850 pages in the volume deal with this question.

Marx's awareness of the relationship between the analyses of the interest rate and of the business cycle is clearly stated, even if his initial analysis of the interest rate disregarded certain complications arising in the context of the business cycle. For example, in the introductory paragraph of Chapter XXII, entitled 'The distribution of the profit. The rate of interest. The "natural" rate of interest', Marx stressed that at first he disregards 'shorter fluctuations' in the money market, and that he does not attempt to analyse the cyclical movement of the interest rate. As can be seen from the text below, he provides two reasons for this: first, the need to start by analysing the cycle itself (a task for which he at that time, and even later, was not yet ready in our opinion); and second, the need to introduce the world market into the analysis. We believe that this joint reference to the business cycle and to the world market is another circumstantial supporting factor for our view that the analysis of the business cycle, together with the analysis of international trade, would have been the concluding joint elements of the picture Marx intended to provide about the total process of capitalist reproduction. But he had not reached that stage yet, at least not as he was writing the text which became chapter XXII:

> The representation of the circulation of interest rate during the industrial cycle presupposes the representation of the cycle itself, and the latter cannot be considered here. The same applies to the more or less, approximate, equalization of the interest rate on the world market.[17]

Notwithstanding his stated desire to disregard the various phases of the movement of interest rates during the cycle, this particular chapter of *Das Kapital* does contain some references to this theme:

> If one considers the cycles, in which modern industry moves – pause [verbatim: the state of rest], increased liveliness, prosperity, over-production, crash, stagnation, pause [verbatim:state of rest] the further analysis of which is out of the scope of our treatment, one finds that mostly low levels of interest corresponds with periods of prosperity and extra profits; rising interest corresponds to the transition from prosperity to the downturn; and the maximum rate of interest up to extremely usurious highs signals the crisis. From the summer of 1843 on there was clearly prosperity; the interest rate fell from $4^1/2\%$ in the spring of 1842 to 2% in the spring and summer of 1843; even to $1^1/2\%$ in September . . . then increased to 8% and more during the crisis of 1847. But it is also true that low interest can go together with stock-building and moderately rising interest with increasing liveliness. The interest reaches its maximum height during the crises, when one must borrow, and to pay whatever it may cost.[18]

The editing of the third volume by Engels
After the death of Marx the second and third volumes of *Das Kapital* were edited and published by Engels on the basis of an incomplete manuscript. Engels made a very extensive effort to accomplish this task and it is not our intention to question his contribution. Indeed without the continuous help of Engels during Marx's lifetime and thereafter – including his financial support to Marx for

many years – the edifice of Marxian political economy would probably have remained much more incomplete. Yet from the viewpoint of the history of economics the difficulties, uncertainties, and unavoidable judgemental decisions of the editor, performing his posthumous work, cannot be disregarded. We venture to say that in the decades to follow those who treated the Marxian political economy as a more finished product than it actually was, would have fared better had they absorbed the significance of these limiting circumstances and had they paid more attention to the caveats implicit in the references of Engels to this matter.

In our review only a few relevant points are considered. We mention only those which are potentially closest to the eventual mathematical–statistical treatment of the business cycle by Marx. Thus, only Engels's editing of the manuscripts related to this subject are considered. Clearly Engels made many other editorial decisions about the third volume which were also important for *Das Kapital* as a whole, but none the less fall outside the scope of this review.

The discussion by Marx of the transformation of surplus value into profit and the transformation of the rate of surplus value into the rate of profit deserves perhaps first mention from the viewpoint of our study. In 1894, in his introduction to the third volume of *Das Kapital*, Engels wrote the following:

> For the first part the main manuscript was useful only with great limitations. At the very beginning the whole mathematical calculation of the relationship of the rate of surplus value and rate of profit is pulled in (what makes our Chapter 3 now), while the subject developed in our Chapter 1 is treated only later and secondarily … Chapter 2 is taken from the main manuscript. For Chapter 3 there were a whole series of incomplete mathematical elaborations, as well as a whole, almost complete note-book from the 1870s, which demonstrate the relationship of the rate of surplus value in equations. My friend Samuel Moore, who also provided the largest part of the English translation of the first book, has taken over to work through the note-book, for which he, as an old Cambridge mathematician was far better prepared than I. Then I completed Chapter 3 from his resumé, from time to time using the main manuscript.[19]

At the end of Chapter 3, Engels provided an additional footnote on this matter:

> In the manuscript there are still very detailed calculations about the difference between the rate of the surplus value and the rate of profit ($m'-p'$), which has all kinds of interesting features; its movement shows the cases, in which the two rates move away or come nearer to each other. These movements can also be represented in curves. I avoid the presentation of this material as it is not so important for the immediate purpose of this book, and simply call this point to the attention of those readers who wish to follow up the matter. F.E.[20]

Only parts of the Marx manuscripts referred to by Engels are in the Amsterdam archives (those marked A 55, A 56, and A 57). However, the manuscript of the summary written by Samuel Moore, which is mentioned in Engels's introduction to the third volume of *Das Kapital* and referred to above, is in Amsterdam. It is essentially a long letter by Moore to Engels, which is of interest mainly in two regards. First, it provides insight into the influence of Moore on the formulation of the given chapter of *Das Kapital*. Second, it supplements our understanding regarding the co-operation of Moore and Marx in mathematics. Here, however, we deal only with one aspect of this communication: the approach taken by Moore in attempting to meet Engels's needs. In this regard, the letter datelined Manchester, 23 March 1888, indicates the following:

> My dear General,
> I return you Marx's MS on Mehrwertsrate + Profitrate mathematisch behandelt together with my notes and an attempt at an analytical summary, which latter is anything but satisfactory – although he, no doubt had a general scheme, which he adhered to in its main outlines, yet in details there appear to be considerable deviations – and there is a great deal which he appears to have written with a view to lighting upon some result – that might be of importance ... I assume that you wish to give what is retained in Marx's own words, and not to give a condensed summary of his results in your own words.[21]

Since only a part of the relevant Marx manuscripts are available, it is not certain exactly which discourses of Marx were disregarded in the editing process. As far as Moore was concerned, he seemed to imply in the letter to Engels that it was not clear to him what 'a great deal' in the manuscript 'intended to light upon' though he surmised that it 'might be of importance'. Engels, on the other hand, relied mostly on Moore in the handling of this matter. Is it possible that attempts by Marx at the treatment of the 'mathematical laws' of the cycle were part of the materials left out? Reading Engels's footnote at the end of chapter 3 of the third volume does not suggest this; none the less, Engels (perhaps even more so than Moore) considered the parts left out of sufficient interest to call the reader's attention to them. It is conceivable that Moore was inclined to disregard materials in the Marx manuscripts pertaining to the mathematical laws of the cycle. After all, fifteen years earlier – according to the letter of 31 May 1873 – he advised Marx about the rather impossible nature of those explorations. At any rate such texts, even if they existed, may have been incomplete, fragmentary, and perhaps just unconvincing to Moore.

Conclusion
Econometrics, the child of the 1930s, and the result of work by Ragnar Frisch, Jan Tinbergen and many other researchers, has been an outstanding effort in our century to provide a modelling framework for macroeconomic relationships. It effectively combined theoretical economics (albeit rarely the Marxist varieties) with mathematical methods and economic and social statistics. Its success – although certainly not a complete one regarding forecasting the business

cycle – was greatly fostered by the computer revolution of our age. Marx's foresight regarding the promise held by such an approach may deserve attention when the history of econometrics is considered.

However, the difficulties (statistical, mathematical, and computational) in adopting an econometric approach in Marx's time were still overwhelming. First, mathematics at the time was considerably less advanced than it is today. In Marx's age important mathematical tools such as matrix algebra, and the advanced statistical techniques which enable economists today to study the structure and the dynamics of economic processes (time series analysis, complex regression techniques, spectral analysis, etc.) were not yet available. Second, economic statistics were very scarce even for England, the most advanced economy of the time. Not only were national accounts non-existent with such indicators as the Gross National Product and its aggregate components, but even price indexes and other basic measures were yet to be developed according to our current understanding of such statistical series. Third, even if both mathematics and data sources had been at a more satisfactory level, the lack of computers, which are now standard tools of economics, would have prohibited carrying out Marx's ambitious undertaking.

Also, while Marx was interested in statistical data applications to economic analysis, his inclination towards probabilistic approaches in economic reasoning (in contrast to deterministic modelling) is unclear. From his philosophical studies, as well as from certain descriptive parts of his socio-economic writings, a degree of understanding of probabilistic processes may be inferred (particularly regarding the relationship of chance and deterministic causation). While, as mentioned, in the nineteenth century advanced econometric techniques were lacking, none the less a degree of probabilistic thought was involved as early as 1838 in Augustin Cournot's mathematical economics and also in Adolphe Quetelet's (1796–1874) social statistical work (including the famous 'average man'). Whether or not Marx was interested in the utilization of such probabilistic strains of thought in his project of combining economics, mathematics, and economic data is, in our view, unclear. Hence, the important probabilistic element in later econometrics may have not been present in his efforts.

Of course, despite the considerable advances in probabilistic approaches to economic analysis, even by the end of the twentieth century there are no completely satisfactory macroeconomic models (non-Marxist or Marxist) that can appropriately explain the business cycle. It is still difficult to forecast accurately the timing of the business cycle, which was a major concern for Marx. As we have seen, for example, the letter of 31 May 1873 placed the forecasting of the business cycle high on his agenda. Hence the timing difficulties of forecasters today are not irrelevant to his plight. Some may even argue that the history of economic forecasting since Marx's time does not offer a great deal of support to Marx's apparent belief in the theoretical feasibility of forecasting efforts.

Whatever we think about the ultimate feasibility of economic forecasting, in our opinion the statistical, mathematical, and computational limitations of the nineteenth century presented major intellectual obstacles to the completion of *Das Kapital* by Marx, especially concerning the analysis and presentation of the business cycle. Other factors, such as ill health, pecuniary problems, family tribulations, and time-consuming political activities – the factors recognized earlier as preventing the completion of *Das Kapital* – quite likely did play a role in delaying Marx. The many years spent on mathematical studies and reviews of data for countries, however, provide important evidence for Marx's intellectual aspirations to elaborate his economics and the cycle in mathematically formulated economics underpinned by actual statistical data.

Finally, we return to the broader implications of the insufficient attention accorded in the past to the incomplete nature of *Das Kapital*. This problem with Marx's *magnum opus*, if given adequate thought, perhaps could have cautioned adherents to his thoughts against handling the economics of Marx in an idolatrous manner. Indeed the history of the three volumes of *Das Kapital*, especially against the backdrop of current developments in Eastern Europe, seems to offer a cautionary conclusion. It clearly warns against treating the works of any human as more than partial triumphs, and monuments of intellectual efforts which will surely be surpassed by later generations.

Notes

1. The author is Senior Economist, Board of Governors of the Federal Reserve System, Washington, DC, USA. The views expressed are entirely personal and are not to be attributed to the Board or its staff.
2. Kolakowski, L. (1978). According to Kolakowski 'There is abundant evidence that all social movements are to be explained by a variety of circumstances and that the ideological sources to which they appeal, and to which they seek to remain faithful, are only one of the factors determining the form they assume and their patterns of thought and action. We may therefore be certain in advance that no political or religious movement is a perfect expression of that movement's "essence" as laid down in its sacred writings; on the other hand these writings are not merely passive, but exercise an influence of their own on the course of the movement. What normally happens is that the social forces which make themselves the representatives of a given ideology are stronger than the ideology, but are to some extent dependent on its own tradition' (Vol. I, pp. 2–3). Kolakowski himself has not 'absolved' Marx by pointing to the complexity of the problem. Indeed his work was 'an attempt to analyse the strange fate of an idea which began in Promethean humanism and culminated in the monstrous tyranny of Stalin' (Vol. I, p. 5).
3. Marx (1954), p.221. Passage translated into English by Z.K. The words 'for the time being' in the last sentence, and the words 'ups and downs' in the previous one are in English in the otherwise German text. Samuel Moore, trained in Cambridge, advised both Marx and Engels on matters of interest to them; he also translated the first volume of *Das Kapital* into English.
4. Koshimura, S. (1986), pp. 2–3. Koshimura sources the quote from Marx on science and mathematics as follows: Lafargue, P., *Karl Marx, Personliche Erinnerungen, Neue Zeit,*

IX. Jahrgang, (1890/91), 'Karl Marx als Denker, Mensch und Revolutionar', *Marxistische Bibliothek*, vol. 4, ed. von D. Rjazanov, p. 98.

5. Mandel, E. (1987), Vol. 3, p. 369.
6. Kenessey, Z. (1962), pp. 195–211, in German; also appeared in Hungarian and Rumanian.
7. Manuscripts of Marx are mostly in German and in a rather difficult to read handwriting in the old Gothic script. However, the notebooks in question were maintained by Marx in English, reflecting not only the place where they were compiled (London, presumably in the Library of the British Museum) but also the availability of English sources for data and news. Thus both the designations of the books and the classification system of the second book are in Marx's handwriting, in Latin script, and in English.
8. The Exchange of colonial goods and other products in England. For lack of a convenient common name for this group of items, Marx designated it after the Exchange.
9. Marx–Engels, (1954), p. 77. Translation into English by Z.K.
10. Marx, K. and Engels, F. (1949), Vol. II, p. 323. Translation into English by Z.K. The last five words in this quotation are in English in the otherwise German text. Among the materials in Amsterdam which pertain to France, the table showing the fluctuations of the discount rate of the Bank of France between 1800 and 1856 is probably the most interesting from the viewpoint of our topic (B 86).
11. Marx, K. and Engels, F. (1961), vol. 12, p. 571. Translation into English by Z.K.
12. Marx, K. and Engels, F. (1949), vol.II, p. 297. Translation into English by Z.K.
13. Marx, K. and Engels, F. (1956), p. 73. An elaborate study of the overall plan, especially regarding the volumes which ultimately appeared, is in R. Rodolsky (1968).
14. Marx, K. and Engels, F. (1954), p. 278.
15. A long laudatory statement by Marx in the introduction to the first volume of *Das Kapital* regarding the evidence on social, economic and health conditions of England collected by parliamentary commissions and other means includes the following statement: 'In comparison with the social statistics in Britain, those of Germany and the rest of western continental Europe are wretchedly compiled.' Marx, K. (1933), p. 863.
16. Marx, K. (1933).
17. Marx, K. (1949), vol.III, p. 391.
18. Marx, K. (1949), vol. III, p. 394.
19. Marx, K. (1949), vol.III, pp. 5–6. The subject Engels decided to treat first was cost, price, and profit; the main manuscript by Marx started with the transformation of surplus value into profit. The reference to Moore as 'an old Cambridge mathematician' should be treated with caution. Samuel Moore (1838–1911) graduated from Cambridge University with a B.A. degree in 1862. He was involved in the cotton spinning business in Manchester (where presumably his long friendship with Engels began). He became a lawyer and served as chief judge in Nigeria. Moore translated Volume I of *Das Kapital* into English and spoke at Engels's memorial service. He must have possessed some mathematical skills, but probably ought not to be considered a 'professional' in that field.
20. Marx, K. (1949), vol.III, p. 89.
21. In the Amsterdam archive this material is marked A 69. It is entitled 'MS. S. Moore: Mehrwertsrate und Profitrate. Summary of Marx' MS'. The salutation 'My dear General' in the letter to Engels probably expresses Moore's regard concerning Engels's place in the international socialist movement as well as jokingly referring to Engels's interest in military science; in their inner circle Marx was sometimes called 'Moor', and Engles 'General'.

References

Kenessey, Z. (1962), 'Marx und die mathematische Analyse des Zyklus', *Konjunktur und Krise*, Wissenschaftliches Bulletin des Instituts für Wirtschaftswissenschaften, Yr. 6, part 4, Berlin: Deutsche Akademie der Wissenschaften.

Kolakowski, L. (1978), *Main Currents of Marxism*, 3 vols, Oxford: Clarendon Press.

Koshimura, S. (1986), *Fixed Capital and Economic Fluctuations: Theory of Crises and Waves*, Tokyo: Hakuto-Shoboh.

Mandel, E. (1987), 'Marx, Karl Heinrich', *The New Palgrave: a Dictionary of Economics*, London and Basingstoke: Macmillan.

Marx, K. (1933), *Capital*, translated by E. and C. Paul, London: J.M. Dent and Sons.

Marx, K. (1949), *Das Kapital*, Berlin: Dietz Verlag.

Marx, K. and Engels, F. (1949), *Briefwechsel*, Berlin: Dietz Verlag.

Marx, K. and Engels, F. (1954), *Briefe uber 'Das Kapital'*, Berlin: Dietz Verlag.

Marx, K. and Engels, F. (1956), *Levelek a Tokerol*, Budapest: Szikra.

Marx, K. and Engels, F. (1961), *Werke*, Berlin: Dietz Verlag.

Rosdolsky, R. (1968), *Zur Entstehungsgeschichte des Marxschen* Kapital, Frankfurt: Europa Verlag. Translated into English in Burgess, P. (1989), *The Making of Marx's 'Capital'*, second (unabridged) paperback edition in two volumes, London: Pluto Press.

10 The defeat of Marxism as economics: the Swedish example

Johan Lönnroth[1]

> The right man was at the right place at the right time ... if you are too far away from a social movement, you rarely have the interest or the competence to appraise it.
>
> Paul Samuelson[2]

Marxism mitigated by God

Marx and Engels came early to Sweden: in 1847, Swedish communists organized the publication of a preliminary draft of the Communist Manifesto. But in order to adapt the pamphlet to the conditions of primitive and conservative Swedish capitalism, some alterations were made. On the front page, 'Proletarians in all countries unite' was replaced by 'The voice of the people is the voice of God'; 'revolution' was toned down to 'radical transformation'; and a passage about feudalism as a past stage of history was deleted. The editor might have thought either that feudalism still existed or that it had never existed at all in Sweden. (Bäckström (1972, p. 81), writes that Per Götrek was the editor. According to Olausson, the text in the Swedish version was written by Carl Rudolf Löwstedt.) With this exception, Marxism was very little known in Sweden during the breakthrough of economic liberalism in the middle of the nineteenth century. Intellectual impulses in political economy came mostly from France with Bastiat as the champion among liberals. It took the combined effect of the publication of the first volume of *Das Kapital* in 1867 and growing German influence after the 1870–71 war for Marx to return.

The first Swedish translation of *Capital* did not come until 1930. For more than 60 years, those Swedes who did not read foreign languages had had to trust second-hand interpretations, mostly by opponents of Marx. The first, in 1873, was a book by the German author Heinrich von Sybel. In an anonymous preface, probably written by the translator 'J.N.N.', the pamphlet was presented as a 'sober and neutral examination' and von Sybel as a man who 'shared Marx's sympathy for the oppressed workers'. The reader was also reminded of a Scandinavian bishop Monrad, who had said that Jesus Christ was the greatest socialist. Von Sybel hardly stimulated his readers to read Marx in the original: 'His style is not agreeable; as a good follower of Hegel, he endeavours to put the vast masses of his material as fragments into one single concept and his reasoning in this way becomes vague, tiresome and heavy'. But von Sybel also admitted that if you accept Marx's premises, you must follow him to the end, 'I will quite intentionally place myself on Marx's own standpoint'. And the standpoint in von Sybel's version was this: the exchange value of a good is a fruit of labour only. Therefore the worker, and not the factory-owner, must have the full legal right to all such value (von Sybel, 1873, p. 7). Out of 'courtesy to Marx', von Sybel supposed that this idea of labour as the only source of value was formed only from the aspect of the sellers' cost. But as everybody knew, the buyer asks if the good can satisfy his enjoyments and needs. Therefore it was untrue that labour is the only source of value. Marx also forgot, wrote von Sybel, that the 'mental work' of the factory-owner is the real master in the production of both value and surplus value. At this point the translator intervened in a footnote, saying that von Sybel here went too far in his eagerness to disprove the socialists (von Sybel, 1873, p. 26). According to von Sybel, Marx's theorem of surplus value was the hinge of his whole theory, so if this idea is falsified, the whole Marxist system tumbles down. And Marx believed – as did the free-traders of the Manchester school – that the state could do nothing against the natural development of capitalism. He therefore had no remedy for the evils of society, which in von Sybel's opinion must be overcome by social reform and 'indefatigable love for mankind' (von Sybel, 1873, p. 78).

In a series of articles in the Swedish journal *Stockholms Morgonblad* in 1873–74, a Swedish author, Carl von Bergen, used von Sybel and other German writers to introduce Marx to a broader Swedish audience. According to von Bergen, the 'Archimedian point' in Marx's system was the doctrine of labour as the sole source of exchange value. The followers of Marx asked if profit is not stolen labour and if the worker did not have a natural right to all wealth. Adam Smith, who proved labour to be the source of all wealth, also bore a certain responsibility for this 'social democratic interpretation'. The Smith connection thus gave a 'scientific shimmer' to Marx (von Bergen, 1881, p. 151). According to von Bergen, the exploitation of labour was an 'outrageous injustice', and Marx wanted to end it by getting rid of the capitalists. This was the main conclusion of the doctrine 'with its pretensions to infallibility'. But was this really the solution of the social problem? Von Bergen's answer was a clear-cut no, since Marx had not in his narrow materialism understood the importance of leadership and 'spiritual power'. The solution was instead that production should be organized as a military unit, with the soldiers and the leader united in a 'brotherhood in arms for a glorious cause' (von Bergen, p. 171).

During the 1880s, several other anti-Marxist and anti-socialist popular pamphlets in the same spirit as von Sybel's and von Bergen's were distributed in Sweden. But now also heavier artillery was mobilized on both sides of the barricade.

Marx in social democracy and at the masters' desk

At the end of the 1870s, the Swedish economy was hit by lower prices for wood and iron. In 1879 the first major strike broke out and in 1881 social democracy was imported from Germany via Denmark by the immigrant tailor August Palm. In 1885 he started a weekly journal, *Socialdemokraten*, soon to be the leading mouthpiece for the movement. There he published the first Swedish party programme, almost literally taken from the German and Lasalle inspired Gotha-programme with its famous opening sentence about labour as the only source of wealth.

The early Swedish workers' movement had poor relations with academic economics, at this time integrated into the faculty of Law. In an unsigned editorial in December 1885, Palm identified 'national-economics' (a literal translation of the Swedish term) with capitalism and wrote in his journal, 'National-economics tramples the theorems of mechanics and physiology under its feet when it appropriates more labour power from the worker than the amount compensated by the wage'. Palm also attacked 'Jeremias' Bentham for his defence of the right to take interest as a human right.[3]

The autodidact Palm was replaced as editor of the party journal in early 1886 by the natural science student Hjalmar Branting. Soon Branting became the leading figure in the movement (and later the first social democratic prime minister). On 24 October 1886 he gave a speech in Gävle, in which he attacked bourgeois economic thought and developed the reasons why the Swedish workers movement should be socialist. He said that it was a direct consequence of free competition that the worker's wages were so low as to be just enough for most basic needs. Capitalist concentration could give a small increase in wages, but in the long run this would not be satisfactory since the workers would become more and more alienated from capitalists (who were both bigger and fewer in number) and socialism would follow as a necessary consequence.[4]

The first professional economist in Sweden to go deeper into the political economy of Marxism was David Davidson, who included a four page footnote about the labour theory of value of the first volume of *Capital* in his dissertation of 1878. There he blamed Adam Smith and his idea about labour as the only source of wealth, for inspiring the socialist theory of surplus labour as the source of capitalist income. Either Smith's theory of value was wrong, or one must admit that the socialist theory was right, wrote Davidson. But nowadays, he argued, we have understood that goods derived from nature (and with no labour spent on them) could have value too (Davidson, pp. 22–7).

When another university teacher in economics, Johan Leffler, presented an obituary for Marx at the *Nationalekonomiska Föreningen* in April 1883, he maintained that the essence of the labour theory of value was that ' ... the present society offends the rights of labour. ... For Marx capital is the same as power and almost a compulsion to deprive the labourer the fruits of his labour'.

But there Marx was wrong, concluded Leffler, 'Because in production capital – that is formerly produced means of production – is also needed. And then the owner of capital must also have a right to his share of the results of production'.[5]

Davidson and Leffler were both on the board of the Lorén Foundation, granting money for students of economics to study abroad. One beneficiary was Knut Wicksell, at this time known as a neo-Malthusian left-winger and a radical opponent of royalty, the church and the sword. In a lecture in November 1886 for a liberal workers association in Stockholm, Wicksell attacked Marxism. Branting responded in *Socialdemokraten*

> that it is a pity to have to count a man like Wicksell with his materialist conception of life as an opponent of social democracy. But as a national-economist he regrettably belongs to the school of Mill and Spencer, which has got stuck in the empirical analysis and not been able to make a synthesis.[6]

Later that month Wicksell gave another lecture. According to a report by Branting, Wicksell then criticized the Swedish socialists for underestimating the threat of over-population and he also attacked the Marxist labour theory of value for neglecting nature as a source of wealth (just as Davidson had done, see p. 136). One can read between the lines that Branting considered Wicksell to be a formidable opponent.[7]

Wicksell versus Wermelin

Probably the only party ideologist who tried to formulate an independent interpretation of Marxist political economy during the pioneering years of the 1880s was the journalist, poet and Bohemian Atterdag Wermelin. He was offended by Wicksell's attack on Marx and he challenged him in a public advertisement in *Socialdemokraten*. So a debate between the two was organized in the Workers' Association in Stockholm. Branting was secretary of the meeting and he prepared a very detailed review for the party journal.[8]

According to Branting, Wermelin opened the debate by stating that Wicksell had attacked the 'popular form' of Marx's 'fundamental statement' about labour as the source of wealth instead of its 'scientific form', which was that 'labour was the source of all wealth *in its social form – its value*' (Branting's emphasis). Wermelin also said that Marx was fully aware that nature was also needed to produce 'use values'. Wicksell replied that this 'scientific' form of the statement was wrong too and that if nature is the mother of production, labour is at most 'the small boy holding on to his mother's apron strings'. He continued by arguing that Marx was wrong when he claimed that 'use value and exchange value were incomparable' and that utility and scarcity – and not just labour – had an influence on exchange value. One can understand that, Wicksell said, by considering the rising price of cotton after a bad harvest. Wicksell also denied that capitalists necessarily always exploit workers, citing as an example a capitalist investing in a virgin forest in the north of Sweden and thereby creating new jobs and new income for the population. Wermelin replied that, if satisfaction really was a part of the determination of value, it could only give 'relative', but not 'absolute' value. He also had difficulties with the cotton example, although he knew little about this. Concerning Wicksell's example of the capitalist in the north, Wermelin noted that the people themselves could just as well have started production without a capitalist. An angry worker intervened, claiming that Wicksell's Malthusianism implied 'a society after the example of bees and ants, where a small minority could have children and where the rest were infertile and a working bunch of slaves'. Another opponent asserted that Wicksell had forgotten to ask how the capitalist got his capital. August Palm, also present at the meeting, said that 'it was clear as the sun' that labour alone is the source of wealth. And Axel Danielsson, later to become the main author of the 1897 party programme, stated that Wicksell's Malthusian ideas would be of good use to the bourgeoisie in suppressing the revolution.

The discussion ended at half past twelve after the chairman had pointed out that Wicksell had not answered the question of whether or not he wanted nature to be publicly owned. Wermelin probably felt that he had lost the debate, at least in the eyes of Branting and the intellectual part of the audience. In 1887 he wrote a pamphlet about the value theory of Marx, in which he tried to provide a better answer to Wicksell: The phrase 'Labour is the source of all wealth' was only: ' ... a popular expression intended to make the hearts of the millions beat' (Wermelin, 1887, p. 8). Wermelin's new pamphlet was reviewed by Branting. He was evidently not impressed and wrote that the 'truth of socialism' was not necessarily coupled to the theory of value. The socialist conception of life was in his opinion more based on the 'necessary development of history' than on 'abstract economics', and 'I for my part', wrote Branting, 'think that it rests safer in that way'.[9]

The law of value and marginalism

In the late 1880s, social democracy grew. In 1889 the party was officially founded. Axel Danielsson, imprisoned for blasphemy (a fate that Wicksell would share a few years later), celebrated the event in jail by writing a pamphlet on the Marxist labour theory of value. He observed that he was aware that price and value seldom coincide, but this was no problem, since the same type of relation between 'law and phenomenon' exist in natural science. In crystallography, for example, in the real world there are always small deviations from the theory, but this does not disprove the natural laws (Danielsson, pp. 17–20). Danielsson also discussed the socialist system of Rodbertus, 'the father of Prussian state socialism'. Rodbertus wanted to introduce 'labour-money' in the form of certificates issued by the state in compensation for labour time which could be used as a means of payment in state-owned shops.

Danielsson considered this system to be Utopian, since only 'free competition' could realize the 'law of labour-time' in the mechanism of exchange. By this he meant that demand and supply determined prices, but behind those forces was a 'higher law' that forced prices to fluctuate around production cost (Danielsson, pp. 23–4).

Danielsson founded the journal *Arbetet* in Malmö in 1887 and one of his foreign correspondents was Gustaf Steffen, also a beneficiary of support from the Lorén foundation (see p. 137). Steffen was later immortalized as a dogmatic socialist in a short story by August Strindberg, with whom he had travelled in France and in vain tried to convert to socialism. Steffen studied with Wagner and Schmoller in Berlin, and moved to London in 1887 where he made contact with Philip Wicksteed and the Fabian Society. His political opinions were influenced by them all.[10]

Steffen soon became the leading interpreter in the Swedish press of neo-classical and Fabian criticism of the labour theory of value. In 1890 he wrote a pamphlet on 'Jevonism', in which he exhorted the Marxists to listen to the new signals. In 1892 he also delivered lectures at University Hall in London about labour economics and labour movements, advocating social reform in the spirit of the German historical school's type of state socialism. The lectures were reported in Sweden in a stream of articles in the social democratic and liberal press.

In 1892 Branting was ready to collect his own thoughts on political economy in an ambitious brochure. He referred to Steffen and took up Jevons's and Böhm-Bawerk's new theory of value which he described as being 'embraced by the majority in the scientific world'. Branting concluded that under free competition Marx's law of value would 'almost' hold true, but that price would also follow the rules set up by Jevons. Among the followers of this new theory one could find 'full-blooded socialists' as well as social reformers. Branting chose not to go into the question of how the Marxists might answer the Jevonists, arguing that the issue was not very important because Engels once said that Marx had not based his demand for socialism on the labour theory of value (Branting, 1906, p. 68).

Branting in 1896 became the first social democratic member of parliament. In 1897 a new party programme was produced, this time mainly inspired by the German Erfurt-programme. But by contrast with its German counterpart, the concepts of surplus value and exploitation were not used. In a speech to a student club with Wicksell as chairman in 1900, Branting spoke in favour of Bernstein's right to express his views. It was not yet a clear stand for revisionism. But that was soon to come (Bäckström, 1971, p. 277).

The professors of economics take over

'Nationalekonomi' was established as a separate academic discipline in Sweden with one chair, in 1903 in Göteborg, and two in 1904 – in Lund and Stockholm. It is a remarkable fact that the first holders – Steffen, Wicksell and Gustav Cassel respectively – were all beneficiaries of the Lorén foundation. In addition, at the turn of the century, all three of them were perceived as sympathetic to some form of socialism, or at least as being close to the workers' movement. Steffen later became a right wing social democrat, Wicksell kept his Malthusianism and left wing liberalism, and Cassel in later years became an outspoken conservative and an ardent anti-socialist. But, before that, all three helped to defeat revolutionary Marxism in Sweden.

Cassel, in an article in 1899, held that it was difficult to attack Marx, who had said very little about what he meant by socialism. Instead Cassel analysed what he took to be the more interesting sort of socialism in its 'modern German meaning' (by which he meant the state-socialist system of Rodbertus). (There was no indication in the article that Cassel was aware of Danielsson's critique of Rodbertus, see p. 138). Cassel's main point of criticism was that Rodbertus thought that wages would follow labour content in his socialist system and that he therefore had not understood the nature of 'scarcity-rent' (Cassel, 1899).

Cassel returned to the problem of distribution under socialism in 1901, when he referred to Bernstein, 'who wanted to raise the proletariat to the level of the bourgeoisie and not the other way around as Marxists normally wanted'. Even Engels had said that it should be possible to get rid of class differences without a decline in total production. But according to Cassel, statistics from Prussia showed that it was impossible to increase the standard of living for the working class by taking money from the rich, since this would damage capital accumulation. Only when the worker himself learned to form capital could 'emancipation in real-economic terms' come (Cassel, 1901, p. 130).

Wicksell became the founding father of neo-classical economics in Sweden. In a paper published in 1899, he sought to 'even out the contradictions between the socialists and the new theory'. In Wicksell's opinion, Marx was correct that capital had its origin in labour and not in the thriftiness of capitalists. But this was a problem only of 'ethical and social interest'; from 'an economic perspective', it was uninteresting (Wicksell, 1899).

In his lectures as a professor, Wicksell sharpened his position: Marx had led the Social Democrats along 'the wrong track'. Why should workers and employers not agree on the price of labour, as sellers and buyers do with other goods? Marxism made the social democrats indifferent to economic reforms. And this was dangerous for the working-class at a time when the number of monopolies and cartels was growing, a phenomenon which, according to Wicksell, showed that 'socialist planning' was gradually growing within the framework of capitalism (Wicksell, 1902 and 1905).

Steffen collected the lectures and articles from his German and English periods in a heavy work published in 1900. There he wrote that Marxism was a doctrine for a 'narrow workers' socialism' during its 'primitive stage', when its leaders were 'agitators and bitter enemies of the higher classes'. In its more 'mature' form, socialism got leaders who are 'social scientists or politicians' (Steffen, 1900, p. 192). In Steffen's opinion, this mature form of socialism must reject the labour theory of value. Marx drove Ricardo's theory 'in absurdum' when he was making labour the source of all wealth and drawing 'the false conclusion that the capitalist was unnecessary'. Marxism also grossly underestimated the spiritual resources of the working class and the importance of moral qualities in modern society (Steffen, 1900, pp. 240–2).

In a review of Werner Sombart's *Kapitalismus* in 1904, Steffen agreed with the German author that labour value was not a measure of exchange value, but a 'theoretical construction outside the consciousness of the capitalist' and that such an 'objective' method in principle was necessary. The pure economic man was a fiction and the 'subjectivism' of marginalism must be complemented with an historical and ethnographical method. But Steffen could not understand why Sombart defended the Marxist labour theory of value in itself, which was 'materially false' (Steffen, 1904, pp. 493–5).

In 1914, Steffen summarized his opinions on Marxism: 'Marx was right that capitalist private property must yield to economic citizenship for the proletariat'. But Marx was wrong if he believed that the proletariat was capable of power and leadership. The reform of private ownership was a 'means' and not an 'end' for the socialist. Therefore socialists must prepare for socialism within the boundaries of capitalism (Steffen, 1914, pp. 87 and 138).

Heckscher versus Höglund, 1908
In 1908, an associate professor of economics, Eli F. Heckscher – later to become the grand old man of Swedish economic history – took up the attack on Marxism in public lectures and articles. Rejoinders to his position were published in *Socialdemokraten* and Heckscher challenged leading social democrats to an open debate. The challenge was taken up and a public debate was held in Stockholm on 7 February 1908.

Heckscher began by saying that for him Marx's theory of capital was dead and that no professional economist wanted to defend it. The point of departure for this theory was the popular formulation of labour as the source of all wealth. This theorem was false in itself. Nobody any longer believed, for example, that a piece of gold or iron ore had its origin in human labour (*Socialismens Grundvalar*, pp. 13–14). According to Heckscher, the materialist conception of history was the simplistic notion that 'conditions of production are the reason for everything'. It was the mark of 'half-education' to try to think of as few things as possible at the same time. Marx had said that the rich would become ever richer and the poor ever poorer. But the workers had become better off and the middle class was not disappearing. Heckscher also provoked part of the audience, including Branting, by saying that the party leader himself agreed with him, even if Branting expressed himself in a vague manner (op. cit., pp. 15–20).

The only reasonably effective reply to Heckscher's attack was delivered by Z. Höglund, chairman of the social democratic youth organization. He asserted that Heckscher was bold when referring to Marx as 'half-educated', when 'Marx's ideas lived while bourgeois economists have been forgotten'. Höglund reminded the audience that Marx himself had once said that he was no Marxist and he vindicated the materialist conception of history as a 'method more than a theory'. The statement about the rich getting richer and the poor poorer must be admitted to be wrong, but the statement could be found only in the Communist Manifesto of 1848 and not later (op. cit., p. 66).

Positivism and Marxism

Axel Hägerström was the founder of the 'Uppsala school', the Swedish version of analytical positivism. He was considered to be close to socialism in his political outlook, but he accused Marxism of being a 'social teleology'. But Hägerström also defended Marxism against the common accusation that it was entirely deterministic. Treating politics as a part of the 'superstructure' and as only a passive reflection of economic conditions was, according to Hägerström, 'a complete distortion of the Marxist theory'. Instead there was a more or less conscious tendency in Marxism to create an *esprit* for the proletariat. This was just an example of the everyday experience in which human beings attempted to construct reality in accordance with their wishes (Hägerström, p. 18).

One of the followers of Hägerström in his ambition to change Marxism in a normative direction was Nils Karleby in his *Socialismen inför verkligheten* (Socialism Facing Reality) of 1926. The author tried to create a compromise between 'subjectivist economics' and 'Marxist sociology'. The latter shaped the background and the 'frame', the former shaped the 'scientific content'. But Karleby referred to Böhm-Bawerk as vindicating the view that workers were exploited by capitalists, since they were unable to wait for their wages. The workers were paid in 'present-values', while the capitalist got less valuable 'future-values'. This value-analysis was, in Karleby's view, in principle the same as that of Marx, even though it led to the conclusion that exploitation in a certain sense was 'fair' (Karleby, p. 182 and pp. 197–9).

According to Karleby, to the degree that the working class participated in social life, capitalism in Marx's sense of the word ceased to exist. This also meant that interest ceased to be a means of exploitation and instead became a necessary instrument for pricing, choice of factor combinations, and accumulation. Crises could be avoided through the choice of a 'proper rate of discount' and by 'correcting purchase power' (Karleby, pp. 209–10 and 277–8).

Karleby died soon after the publication of the book. He was followed as leading party ideologist in economic matters by Ernst Wigforss, an outspoken revisionist Marxist, when he published a book on the materialist conception of history in 1908. In 1932 Wigforss became minister of finance and a leading symbol for the new economic policies of the 1930s. In his autobiography, he later confessed that his Marxism was inspired by Sombart more than by Marx. In any case, his earlier theoretical involvement did not prevent him from being the leading spokesman for Keynesianism in Sweden (Wigforss, 1970, and p. 271 in 1950).

The professional economists in the group that would later be called the Stockholm school of economics were definitely not Marxists. One of them, Gunnar Myrdal, advocated openly declared value judgements and for an 'ends and means' type of normative economics. He also attacked 'metaphysical' concepts like utility and labour value. In 1931 he wrote that Marxism was based on a 'philosophy of natural rights' and that the difference between Marxism and eighteenth century thinking was that the former was 'disguised in a historical–philosophical deterministic dogma and deprived of its eighteenth century optimism'. In his inauguration speech as a professor in 1934 he also referred to Marxism as an example of an 'ideological science of totalitarian regimes' and that 'its deterministic dogma had been given its sentence by modern sociology' (Myrdal, 1931, p. 61 and 1934, p. 12).

The labour theory of value as a special case of neo-classical economics

Herbert Tingsten, a social democratic friend of Myrdal's, was inaugurated in 1934 as a professor of political science. He was given the task by the party of writing its ideological history, and in spite of the fact that Tingsten later left the party for the liberals, this was to become the standard work on the subject. Tingsten distinguished between what he called Marx's 'large and small perspectives'. The large perspective contained generalizations about the historical development of mankind and the factors behind the coming revolution. When working within the small perspective, Marx tried to establish the main facts of actual events and the conditions for short-term political change. Then he could not use his large perspective, but he had to change the meaning of its concepts in order to loosen their deterministic implications (Tingsten, part 1, pp. 84–5).

According to Tingsten, the materialist conception of history had its roots in Hegel's metaphysics, and it was impossible to combine it with practical politics. The implication was that only when social democracy chose Keynesianism, with its small perspective, and abandoned the large perspective of Marxism could it develop a consistent and successful political strategy. Tingsten's view on Marxism was to dominate official Sweden with its social democratic hegemony (in Gramsci's meaning of the term) from the beginning of the 1930s through a long period of Social Democratic government. It was not to be challenged until the rise of the 1968 student generation.

The student protest movement provoked a fresh round of debate. Assar Lindbeck, then a professor at the Stockholm School of Economics, took issue with the readings of Marx then propounded by members of the younger generation with the publication of *The Political Economy of the New Left* in 1970. There he wrote that the Marxists in their theories of crisis and imperialism had not understood that nowadays the state can control demand. He also claimed that in the Marxist theory of value, 'profits are never seen as signs of efficiency or as acceptable incentives for innovation or expansion', but only as indications of the degree of exploitation. And this was so even if highly efficient companies paid higher wages (Lindbeck, p. 61). One of the reviewers, Lars Herlitz, took exception. While noting that no Marxist would then deny the roles of capitalist competition and profits in the allocation of investments, Herlitz wrote that he 'was sorry to inform Lindbeck that the power of the state, such as we meet it in reality will not conform to the normative statements from economists'. To understand the state, one must have an historical and economical analysis of property and class conditions in the society. But that type of analysis was excluded in advance in Lindbeck's 'subjectivist instrumentalism' (Herlitz, p. 56).

For a short period at the beginning of the 1970s, Marxism came back as a tolerated element of academic economics in Sweden. But when traditional Keynesianism was crowded out by neo-liberalism, Marxism also gradually disappeared. Only faint complaints were heard from left wing students. Most of them were probably relieved when they no longer needed to grapple with the transformation problem.

A further attempt to accommodate a Marxian perspective with neo-classical doctrine is, however, worth noting. Writing in 1981, Bo Gustafsson – one of the leading Marxists – argued that, while many Marxists used to deny the relevance of non-Marxist economic theory, they now had to accept neo-classical economics as useful for the study of short-term demand and as a complement to the long-term prices which were best analysed from the supply side of the labour theory of value (Gustafsson, 1981, pp. 30–31). Two years later, Gustafsson was prepared to move a step further. Also in the long run, prices could be influenced by the structure of need and preferences. A mutual relation existed between factors deciding values and values themselves in the economy. The labour theory of value could '... simply be seen as a special case of the general supply–demand analysis' (Gustafsson, 1983, p. 178).

The relevance of Marx for economics

There are three important ideas in Marx's writings (for example in *Capital*, part I, chapters 21 and 22), which are still relevant for the critique of modern mainstream economics. Marx is by no means the only inventor of those ideas, but he expressed them best:

1   There is a hidden non-symmetric power-relation behind contracts, which on the surface look as if they are established by free and equal human beings. This idea could be applied to the contract between capitalist and worker or between husband and wife, just to take two examples.
2   You feel alienated in relation to your work when you do not know from where your inputs come or to where your products go.
3   The mind of an owner of private property is split – Marx compares him with Goethe's Faust – between the lust for power and the lust for an agreeable life as a consumer.

But criticism was not enough for most Marxist political economists. Instead they tried to develop Marx's thinking into a positive alternative to the theories of prices and quantities of 'scientific' economics. And since the labour theory of value in its quantitative aspects is not only redundant for the expression of those three mentioned ideas, but also contains many mistakes of a mathematical nature, Marxism was doomed to be defeated as political economy not only for the bourgeoisie, but also for the workers' movement.

In anti-Marxist attacks from mainstream economists, many dirty tricks were used. In contrast to what for example Davidson and Wicksell said, Marx was well aware that nature, and not only labour, is a source of wealth. In the beginning of *Capital* part I, Marx cites Petty, who once said that nature is the mother and labour is the father of material wealth (Marx, 1921, p.10). And in his critique of the Gotha-programme, 1875, Marx also wrote: 'Labour is *not the source* of all wealth. *Nature* is just as much the source of use values (and it is surely of such that material wealth consists!) as labour...' (Marx, 1971, p.11, italics in original).

In contrast to what von Bergen, Lindbeck and others wrote, Marx was also well aware that the capitalist not only 'deducts profits', but that he also plays a role as an entrepreneur in capitalist production. He also often stressed that profits are important incentives for choice of technique and capitalist growth. (See for example the first pages of Marx's commentary to Adolph Wagner's textbook in political economy.)

Marx also knew that short run market prices are decided by the joint forces of supply and demand. But the 'law of value' – the Achilles heel of Marxism – was wrong and on this point Marx himself must be blamed. Labour values are not in any reasonable sense 'centres of gravity' for either production prices or market prices. And this is true even if exchange 'ceases to be purely accidental or merely occasional', if commodities are produced in relative quantities that approximately correspond to the mutual need' and if 'no natural or artificial monopolies enable one of the contracting parties to sell above value, or force them to sell cheap, below value (*Capital* III, pp. 278–9). In Lönnroth (1989), a longer argument against the law of value can be found.'

The concept of labour–value is just as useful or as useless as labour–input–coefficients in modern input–output models. The endless discussions about the transformation problem lead to nothing but a collective inferiority complex among Marxist political economists.

Sweden as a special case

The defeat of Marxism as economics was perhaps more clear-cut in Sweden than in any other country. I think there are two main reasons for this. First, Sweden had peace after 1815; in combination with old traditions of political compromise and peasant morale, this created a less fruitful climate for revolutionaries like Marx. Second, progressive and anti-Marxist economists, particularly with Knut Wicksell, Gunnar Myrdal and Assar Lindbeck, were extremely influential. Wicksell failed to separate Marx from German state socialists. Myrdal and Lindbeck were poor interpreters of Marx and tried to analyse his work through the anachronistic spectacles of narrow instrumentalism. But their legitimacy as progressive chief engineers of the 'Swedish Model' was strong enough to give their anti-Marxism credibility.

Sweden is a small and open economy. Her leading economists in the present century always had close contacts with Anglo-Saxon economics and with the pragmatic and technocratic social democratic and liberal establishments. Their hegemonic ideology left little space for continental type Marxist – and conservative – alternatives. Sweden was not only the 'middle road', but also the kingdom of mainstream economics.

Notes

1. Katarina Katz and Iris Lönnroth have given valuable advice. The commentary by Lars Magnusson on an earlier version of this paper, was also very helpful.
2. 'Foreword', Lindbeck (1970).
3. *Socialdemokraten*, 18 December 1885.
4. 'Varför arbetarrörelsen maste bli socialistisk', in Branting, 1926, p. 91 ff. Evidently Branting at this time had come into contact with Lasalle's 'iron law of wages' rather than the writings of Marx.
5. Protocols from *Nationalekonomiska Föreningens Förhandlingar*, 26 April 1883.
6. *Socialdemokraten*, 5 November 1886, unsigned article that must have been written by Branting.
7. 'Knut Wicksell och socialismen', *Socialdemokraten*, 26 November 1886. The article is reproduced in Branting, 1926, part 1.
8. *Socialdemokraten*, 17 December 1886, read from a microfilmed version at the university library in Göteborg.
9. *Socialdemokraten*, 6 August 1887, cited by Olson, p. 38.

10. A longer article about Steffen can be found in Lönnroth, J., *Ekonomisk Debatt*, no. 3, 1989.

References

Bäckström, K. (1971), *Arbetarrörelsen i Sverige*, del I (*Workers' Movements in Sweden*, Vol. I), Stockholm: Rabén & Sjögren.

Bäckström, K. (1972), *Götrek och manifestet* (*Gotrek and the manifesto*), Stockholm: Gidlunds

Bergen von, C. (ed.) (1881) *Frågor på dagordningen* (*Questions concerning the agenda of the day*), Stockholm: Lönbohms förlag.

Branting, H. (1906), 'Socialismen', *Studentföreningen Verdandis Småskrifter* (*The Student Association Verdandis pamphlets*), 45. (second revised edition, first edition 1892) Bonniers.

Branting, H. (1926), *Tal och skrifter* (*Speeches and writings*), part I and II, ed. Z Höglund and others, Stockholm: Tiden.

Cassel, G. (1899), 'Vetenskapen och det "socialistiska samhället"' ('Science and the socialist society'), *Ekonomisk Tidskrift*.

Cassel, G. (1901), 'Kapitalbildningen och den socialistiska delningstanken' ('Capitalist accumulation and the socialist plan of distribution'), *Ekonomisk Tidskrift*.

Danielsson, A. (1889), *Socialismens Hörnsten*, (Historisk och teoretisk framställning af läran om värdet) (*The Cornerstone of Socialism* (Historical and theoretical account of the theory of value), (pamphlet) Malmö and New York: Arbeterens.

Davidson, D. (1878), *Bidrag till läran om de ekonomiska lagarna för kapitalbildningen* (Contribution to the theory of the economic laws of capital accumulation) Doctoral thesis, University of Uppsala.

Gamby, E. (1983), 'Hantverkskommunismen i Sverige' ('Workers' Communism in Sweden'), *Marx i Sverige* (*Marx in Sweden*), ed. L. Vikström. Stockholm: Arbetarkultur.

Gustafsson, B. (1981), *I övermorgon socialism* (*The Day after tomorrow: Socialism*), Stockholm: Gidlunds.

Gustafsson, B. (1983), *Marx & marxismen* (*Marx and Marxism*), Stockholm: Gidlunds/Verdandi.

Hägerström, A. (1909), *Social teleologi i marxismen* (*Social teleology and Marxism*), Akademiska boktryckeriet, E. Berling: Uppsala.

Herlitz, L, (1971), 'Marxism och instrumentalism' (recension av Assar Lindbeck's *Den nya vänsterns politiska ekonomi*, i häften för kritiska studier nr 3) ('Marxism and instrumentalism' (review of Assar Lindbeck's *Political economy of the new left*), an installment of critical studies no. 3).

Karleby, N. (1926), *Socialismen inför verkligheten* (*Socialism before reality*), Stockholm: Tiden.

Lindbeck, A. (1970), *Den nya vänsterns politiska ekonomi* (*The political economy of the new left*), Stockholm: Bonniers.

Lönnroth, J. (1985), *Minervas Uggla* (*Minerva's Owl*), Stockholm: Arbetarkultur.

Lönnroth, J. (1989), *Politisk Ekonomi* (*Political Economy*), Stockholm: Arbetarkultur.

Marx, K. (1921), *Das Kapital*, I, ninth printing, Hamburg: Otto Meissners Verlag.

Marx, K. (1971), *Critique of the Gotha programme*, (first pub. 1875), Moscow: Progress Publishers.

Marx, K. (1981), *Capital*, III, Harmondsworth: Penguin Books in association with New Left Review.

Myrdal, G. (1931), 'Kring den praktiska nationalekonomins problem', ('Concerning the practical national economic problem'), *Ekonomisk Tidskrift*.

Myrdal, G. (1934), 'Den förändrade världsbilden inom nationalekonomin' ('The changing world picture within political economy'), (inaugural lecture in company with Herbert Tingsten on 31 March 1934), in *Samhällskrisen och socialvetenskaperna* (The social crisis and the social sciences), Stockholm: KFs förlag.

Myrdal, G. (1961), *The political element in the development of economic theory*, (third impression, first pub. 1953), London: Routledge & Kegan Paul.

Olausson, L. (1980), 'Marxism och Socialdemokrati' (*Marxism and Social Democracy*), *17 uppsatser i svensk idé- och lärdomshistoria* (*17 essays in Swedish on the history of doctrine*), Stockholm: Bokförlaget Carmina.

Olson, J.-E. (1983), 'Atterdag Wermelin och arbetarrörelsen- en biografi' ('Atterdag Wermerlin and the workers' movement: a biography'), in *Marx i Sverige (Marx in Sweden)*, Lars Vikström (ed.), Stockholm: Arbetarkultur.

Persson, C. (1983), 'Marx, Danielsson,Vi' ('Marx, Danielsson, Us'), in *Marx i Sverige (Marx in Sweden)*, Lars Vikström (ed.), Stockholm: Arbetarkultur.

Socialismens Grundvalar (The Foundations of Socialism), (summary of the discussion at the Assembly Hall in Stockholm, 7 February 1908), Stockholm: Socialdemokratiska Arbetarepartiets Bok- och Broschyrförlag.

Steffen, G. (1890), 'Den nya riktningen inom Englands nationalekonomi' ('The new direction of England's political economy'), *Finsk Tidskrift*, Senare halfåret, s 3-18.

Steffen, G. (1900), *Lönearbetaren och samhället (Wage earners and society)*,Stockholm: Bonniers.

Steffen, G. (1904), 'Om det moderna produktionssättets väsen (med särskild hänsyn till Sombarts "Kapitalismus")' ('On the character of the modern mode of production (with special consideration of Sombart's "Kapitalismus")'), *Ekonomisk Tidskrift*, del I s 483–509 och del II s 523–45.

Steffen, G. (1914), *Utvecklingen av Karl Marx' materialistiska samhällsuppfattning (The Development of Karl Marx's materialist conception of society)*, Stockholm: Tiden.

Sybel, H. von (1873), *Den sociala frågan-socialismens och kommunismens läror (The social question: socialist and communist doctrines)*, translated from German by 'J.N.N.', Linköping.

Tingsten, H. (1941), *Den svenska socialdemokratins idéutveckling (The development of Swedish social democratic ideas)*, in two volumes, Stockholm: Tiden.

Wermelin, A. (1887), *Karl Marx' värdeteori (Karl Marx's theory of value)*, Stockholm: Bonniers.

Wicksell, K. (1899), 'Klassisk nationalekonomi och vetenskaplig socialism' ('Classical political economy and scientific socialism'), *Ekonomisk Tidskrift*.

Wicksell, K. (1902), *Allianser mellan arbetare och arbetsgivare (The alliance between workers and employers)*, Stockholm: Verdandis småskrifter.

Wicksell, K. (1905), *Socialiststaten och nutidssamhället (The socialist state and modern society)*, Stockholm: Verdandi.

Wigforss, E. (1950), *Minnen, (Memoirs)*, vol. I, Stockholm: Tiden.

Wigforss, E. (1970), 'Materialistisk historieuppfattning' (The materialist conception of history), (first pub. 1908) in *Materialistisk historieuppfattning, industriell demokrati, (The Materialist conception of history and industrial democracy)*, Stockholm: Tiden.

Name Index

Actes du Colloque International sur
  Averroës, 11
Adkins, A.W.H., 40
Aegidius Romanus, 31
Ahmad, I., 9
Al-Biruni, 7
Al-Dawani, 14, 18
Al-Dimashqi, 7, 8, 15
Al-Farabi, 5, 7, 11
Al-Ghazali, 5, 7, 10–11
Al-Kindi, 5
Al-Maqrizi, 14, 17–18
Al-Raziq, A., 8
Al-Turtushi, 7
Alemannus, Hermannus, 12
Alexander III, Pope, 33
Alexander of Hales, 29
Alexander Lombard, 28, 29–30, 31–2
Allah, 4, 13, 18
Ambrosia, 29
Andic, S., 15
Anspach, R., 62
Antin, Duc D', 56
Aquinas, Thomas, 24–5, 26, 27–8, 29,
  34–5
Aretus, 12
Aristotle, 3, 5–6, 7, 11–12, 13, 18, 24
Arrow, K.J., 71
Ash-Shaybani, 8
Augustine, 29, 35
Avicennes, 5, 11

Bäckström, K., 134, 139
Bacon, Roger, 44
Badawi, A., 11
Baeck, L., 3
Bagehot, Walter, 99, 113
Bensa, E., 32
Bentham, Jeremy, 64, 65, 136
Bernard, A., 25
Bernstein, E., 139, 140
Bigelow, Jacob, 108, 110
Blake, William, 93
Blaug, M., 74

Böhm-Bawerk, E. von, 139, 142
Bonar, J., 73, 74
Boulakia, J., 15
Bousquet, G., 7
Brandon, S.G.F., 42
Branting, H., 136, 137, 138, 139, 142
Brouwer, 67–8, 71
Bryson, 14
Buridanus, 14
Buttenwurth, C., 11

Cairnes, J.E., 85
Campbell, L.B., 44
Campbell, W.F., 62
Cannan, Edwin, 61, 73, 74, 79
Cantillon, Richard, 50, 58, 59
Cassel, Gustav, 140
Chadwick, Edwin, 108–9, 110
Chalmeta, P., 8
Chamberlen, Hugh, 49
Chrysostome, John, 29
Collard, D., 66, 67
Collins, S.L., 45
Constantine, Emperor, 6
Cournot, Augustin, 130
Cyrus the Great, 39

Danielsson, Axel, 138–9, 140
Danner, P.L., 62
Davidson, David, 136, 137, 145
Dawood, A., 7
Dawood, N., 14
Desomogyi, J., 7
Diamond, P.A., 66, 67
Dutot, C., 59

Edgeworth, F.Y., 67, 112, 113
Ekelund, R.B., 84
Engels, Friedrich, *see subject index*
Erasmus, D., 44
Essid, M., 4, 7

Faure, E., 58
Finley, M.I., 40–41

149

Subject Index

Abbasid empire, 7, 8
acquisitions and mergers, 56
administrative efficiency, 40, 45
administrative tradition, 39–46
'agency problem', 28
aggregate demand, 67
aggregate spending, 92
aggregate supply, 67
Al-Maqrizi, 14, 17–18
altruism, 65, 66, 67
analytical positivism, 142
anthropocentric tradition, 44
anti-bullionists, 94–5
anti-Marxism, 135, 145
anti-monetarism, 91, 92, 96, 98–9
anti-Socialist pamphlets, 135
Arbetet (journal), 139
assignats, 49, 59
asymmetric information, 30, 33
'Atlantization', 4
authority, 40, 45
Averröes, 5
    philosophical tradition of, 10–14

balance of payments, 50, 51, 58, 93, 97, 98
Bank of Amsterdam, 54
Bank Charter Act (1844), 97, 106, 110, 111
Bank of England, 50, 53–5, 92–6, 98–9, 106, 110, 111, 112, 113
    Marx and, 122, 123, 125
Bank Restriction period, 92
bank reserves, 91
Bankers' Magazine, 110
banking profession, 105–13
banking school, 106, 110
    -currency school debate, 96–101
banknotes
    Law's policy, 53–5, 58
    overissue, 92, 96–7, 98, 105–6
bankruptcies, 122–3
barter, 51, 93
'benevolence', 43

Bible, 5–6
Billets d'état, 55–6
bills of exchange, 94, 95–6
British Association, 112
British Medical Association, 107
bullionist controversy, 92–6, 106
business cycle, 119, 124–5, 129–30, 131
    interest rate and, 126–7

calculus, 69
capital accumulation, 75, 140
capitalism (Sweden), 134–8, 140–42, 144
capitalists, 83–4, 105
    reproduction cycle, 125, 127
cartels, 140
causality, 91, 92, 97, 98
census (analysis), 28, 31
central banks, 91, 95, 96, 99, 101
Christianity, 4, 5, 6, 11, 41, 134–5
city, organization of, 8–10
clan society, 4
'classical argument', 24
classical controversies (money/banking)
    commercial therapeutics, 105–13
    Kaldor-Friedman debate, 91–101
classical Islam, 19
    crisis literature, 14–18
    golden age, 7–14
    Islam as force in history, 4–7
    Mediterranean tradition, 3–4
classical monetarists, 92–3
classical nonmonetarists, 94–5
classical Platonism, 40–43
classical themes (variations)
    Law's policies, 49–59
    moral sentiments and marketplace, 61–71
    'rigid' wages fund doctrine, 73–85
classical wage theory, 75, 76, 78
commercial banks, 91, 96, 100
commercial therapeutics (Victorian England)
    banking profession, 109–12
    introduction, 105–7

loans, 25, 26–7, 29
  'monster' of, 78–82, 85
  paper, 53, 55, 59, 92
  passive, 98, 101
  -to-price causality, 91, 92
  quantity theory, 50, 101
  recantation and, 83–5
  sterility of, 24
  substitutes, 99, 101
  supply, 51–2, 54–5, 59, 94–5, 97–8
  trade and, 51–2
Money Market Review, 122
Money and Trade Consider'd (Law), 49–54
monopolies, 140
monopolist, 66, 67
monopsonist, 66
'monster-adjustment', 78, 81, 85
'monster-barring', 77, 81, 85
'monster' of money, 78–82, 85
moral hazard, 30, 32, 34–5
moral sentiments, 61–71
moralist, 23–4, 28, 30, 33, 34
morality, 42
muhtasib, 8, 9, 10, 17
multi-reserve system, 111, 113
mutuum, 26, 27, 29, 30, 35

Napoleonic Wars, 96
'national-economics', 136
national budget, 16
national debt, 55–9
national income, 52
natural law, 43, 105, 138
naturalism, 43, 45
Naviganti, 32, 33–4
neo-classical economics, 65, 107, 113, 140, 143–5
neo-liberalism, 144
Neoplatonism, 11
non-tuism, 67
non usurious income, 30–32
non usurious ratio of exchange, 26
normative analysis, 27–8
normative economics, 143

open economy, 45, 145
open market, 91
opportunity cost, 26, 27, 29, 35
ownership transfer, 29, 30

paper money, 53, 55, 59, 92
pareto-optimality, 61, 62, 64, 70, 71
patriarchal authority, 39, 40
penalty (by common agreement), 35
perfect information, 64, 67, 70, 71
physiocrats, 105
Platonism, classical, 40–43, 45
pleasure, 63–4
political economy, 11–12, 44, 109–10
  of Marxism, 128, 136–7, 139, 145
polytheism, 4
popularization, 45
population, 16, 17, 75
positivism, Marxism and, 142–3
poverty, 31
pre-classical economics
  classical Islam, 3–19
  ethical individualism, 39–46
  usury, information and risk, 23–36
present good, 25–6, 27, 31
present values, 142
'presuppositions', 74
price setting, 10
price system, 65
price theory, 7, 16
prices, 97–8
  absolute/relative, 94
  just, 23–4, 26–7
Principles of Political Economy, The (McCulloch), 78–9, 82
probabilistic approaches, 130
production, theory of, 15–16
profit, 8, 26–7, 29, 144
  -maximization, 66, 67
  rate of interest, 95–6
  surplus value and, 128
proletariat, 134, 140, 141, 142
Proofs and Refutations (Lakatos), 74, 75–6, 78, 81
property, 24, 29–32
public interest, 45
purchasing power, 92, 93, 143

quantity theory, 50, 101

Radcliffe Committee (1959), 101
rational efficiency, 41
rational individualism, 39, 40
rationalism, 10–14
rationality, 39, 124–5
  Plato's views, 41, 42–3, 45